Cooking with all Things Trader Joe's

Cookbook

Deana Gunn Wona Miniati

Cooking with All Things Trader Joe's
by Deana Gunn and Wona Miniati
Photographs by Deana Gunn and Wona Miniati
Designed by Lilla Hangay and 2M Creative
Cover design by Lilla Hangay

DISCLAIMER: The information in this book is not intended as medical advice nor intended to cure, treat, or diagnose any ailment or disease. The authors, publishers and/or distributors do not assume responsibility for any adverse consequences resulting from adopting any health information described herein.

Published by Brown Bag Publishers, LLC
P. O. Box 235065
Encinitas, CA 92023-5065
info@cookTJ.com

Printed in Korea through Codra Enterprises, Inc.

Library of Congress Cataloging-in-Publication Data
Gunn, Deana & Miniati, Wona.
Cooking with All Things Trader Joe's /
by Deana Gunn & Wona Miniati: photographs by Deana Gunn & Wona Miniati.-2nd ed.
Includes index.

I. Cooking- Quick & Easy. 2. Trader Joe's (Store) I. Title.

Library of Congress Control Number: 2007906686

ISBN 978-0-9799384-8-1

Contents

Thank You Notes

We are eternally grateful to Cary, Doug, and the kids, who cheerfully sampled and re-sampled many versions of our recipes, from the yummy to the crummy and everything in between. They were also graciously tolerant of large piles of dirty dishes, fridges stuffed to the brim with Trader Joe's jars, and late night photo shoots.

Our parents have always cheered us on in all our endeavors. Thank you for believing in us.

Our cross-country team of enthusiastic testers and advisors includes: Fara Rafizadeh, Neala Rafizadeh, Chris Hofmann, Kerry Crum, Stephanie Bollini, Grady Gunn, Lara Hammock, Andres & Nancy Kohn, Jamie & Keri Hoffacker, Suzanne Jensen, Mark Henderson, Tricia Clarke, and Ben Nemo. Thank you for making time to road test our recipes and improve on them.

Larry Gunn proofread the final draft, patiently editing errors and typos, a job that only a true friend would take on.

Wine connoisseur Rene Geniblazo hand-picked wine pairings for some of our recipes.

Our photographer friends Christina Aris and Loïc Nicolas gave us crash courses in photography, enabling us to jump into amateur food photography almost overnight.

Our creative designer Lilla Hangay designed new covers and layouts for our growing collection of *Cooking with Trader Joe's* cookbooks. We hope you love the new look as much as we do!

We thank Evalyn Carbrey, registered dietitian, and Eddy Kim, nutritionist, for doing all the number-crunching for the nutritional data in this book.

Finally, this book would not have been possible without Trader Joe's stores. Crewmembers at our local stores must have wondered what we were up to as we scribbled feverishly on notepads and walked out with enough food for a week, almost daily. We appreciate your politeness in overlooking the abnormal and greeting us so cheerfully on every visit.

Our heartfelt thanks to you all.

Introduction

Trader Joe's is one of the fastest growing grocery chains in the nation as well as one of the most fun food shopping experiences around. Trader Joe's has all the usual grocery basics but is best known for its array of affordable gourmet foods, wines, cheeses, and ready-to-use items, such as specialty sauces, dips, and prepped fresh ingredients. What more could you ask for? Here is the cookbook, written by Trader Joe's fans, that pulls it all together with recipes and menu ideas using Trader Joe's unique foods.

Let Trader Joe's Be Your Prep Crew

Make the most of the timesaving, prepped ingredients at Trader Joe's stores

At the break of dawn, restaurant kitchens across the country come alive. Prep crews are hard at work, creating sauces, fillings, and mixtures. Later that day, as the lunch and dinner crowds roll in, chefs use these basics to create complex and delicious meals quickly and efficiently. Taking advantage of the prep work, chefs create gourmet magic without the laborious and time-consuming task of doing everything from scratch.

Ever wished you had your own prep crew? Well, you do. At your neighborhood gourmet grocer, Trader Joe's. There you will find unique, fully prepped sauces, washed and cut vegetables, ready-to-use salads, gourmet cheeses, marinated meats, even fully cooked items ready to assemble – from all around the world. The food is delicious and consistently high quality.

Home-cooked gourmet meals with typical working times of around 10 minutes

Cooking with All Things Trader Joe's is here to help you make the most of the timesaving, prepped ingredients at Trader Joe's stores. Our recipes show you how to create delicious, gourmet meals in just minutes by cleverly pairing the right ingredients.

If you're like us, you love to eat natural, delicious, home-cooked foods, but due to career, family, or simply a busy modern lifestyle, you can't make meals from scratch every night. There's a time and place for take-out and frozen entrées, but there's never a substitute for home-cooked meals.

By using fresh ingredients strategically coupled with prepped items, you can have healthy, home-cooked gourmet meals with typical working times of around 10 minutes. We'll show you how.

About Us: The Evolution of Gourmet Cooking

We're Deana Gunn and Wona Miniati. We love good food, we love to cook, and we love Trader Joe's. Over time, we found ourselves wishing that Trader Joe's had a cookbook to go with all their fabulous products. What do you do with quinoa? How do you use tapenade? What goes well with ricotta-stuffed chicken? Before we knew it, we were writing a cookbook.

We grew up in homes where cooking was all-important and meals were always shared at an inviting family table. Given our international backgrounds, we were exposed to various ethnic and American styles of cooking. We met 18 years ago while studying engineering in Boston, where our exposure to food continued to grow, whether it was the spicy Dun Dun noodles at the local hole-in-the-wall Central Square Chinese restaurant or the amazing paella and sangria in Harvard Square.

We would let Trader Joe's be our kitchen prep crew...

Our skill at cooking evolved as we found ourselves out in the real world, recalling old family recipes, experimenting with new ones, and learning the culinary arts through the school of experience. From the neighborhood greasy spoon to the French bistro, we savored the adventure of eating out. But we also wanted to treat ourselves, our friends, and our families to homemade, fresh, and exciting food.

Over time, whether we were students, single, working, married, or mothers, our love for gourmet cooking was continuing to grow, but it was starting to get squeezed out by our busy schedules!

Through necessity, we found ways to be efficient and fast gourmet cooks, without compromising taste or quality. We wanted good food with great quality ingredients, sophisticated yet fun, eclectic yet accessible by everyone in the family. And we wanted gourmet food for *every day*, not just special occasions.

We would be the chefs showing up later in the day to create magic.

Our cooking began to evolve, as we discovered a whole new type of "fusion cooking" using our favorite grocer, Trader Joe's. We would let Trader Joe's be our kitchen prep crew. Basic or unique sauces, ethnic or American, all kinds of fillings and toppings, washed and chopped vegetables, everything we needed and everything prepped. We would be the chefs showing up later in the day to create magic.

About this Book

Several things make this cookbook unique.

First, all of the ingredients in our recipes – yes, all of them – can be found at Trader Joe's. We are big fans of one-stop shopping! Trader Joe's isn't just the best place for wine, cheese, and breads; it has everything a traditional store would stock. So even if your fridge and pantry are bare, fear not, you'll be preparing yummy gourmet meals with just one trip to Trader Joe's.

All ingredients can be found at Trader Joe's

Second, this cookbook didn't come from Trader Joe's. It came from Trader Joe's fans. We've been making many of these recipes for our families for years. Others, we created especially for this cookbook by creating clever shortcuts to lengthy recipes using Trader Joe's prepped products.

Finally, a picture is worth a thousand words, and we think this is even more true for cookbooks. All the photos you see in this cookbook are, well, REAL. No mashed potatoes covered in motor oil posing as ice cream. No meat covered in glycerin to make it look moist and juicy. No chickens blowtorched on the outside but kept raw on the inside to maximize plumpness. Unlike professionally styled food that is often inedible, all the food you see here was prepared in our home kitchens, with no unusual equipment, no chemicals, no smoke and mirrors, and no photo tricks. (And, yes, we ate it all after each photo was taken!)

You asked for nutritional data, and we listened! This revised edition now includes nutritional data for every recipe, as well as a **gluten-free** index and **vegetarian** index – to make it easier to accommodate any dietary restrictions.

Proper names of Trader Joe's items are capitalized in recipes

Proper names of Trader Joe's items are capitalized; generally assume they are shelf-stable (a jarred sauce, for example) unless specified otherwise (frozen, refrigerated). If you're a regular shopper, you already know that some Trader Joe's items are seasonal or discontinued as new items are introduced. For that reason, we offer substitution ideas in case an item is not in stock. We encourage you to experiment and come up with substitutions of your own!

We hope you'll enjoy the recipes, savor the food, impress your friends and family, and then scratch your head figuring out all the great things to do with your extra time!

About Trader Joe's

If you've never shopped at Trader Joe's, you're in for a big treat. You will soon discover the reasons we (and other fans) are so devoted and loyal:

Value and quality. At Trader Joe's, you'll find everything from the very basics to high-end gourmet food at affordable prices. All the food is high quality and delicious, with organic and natural food options found throughout the store.

Unique products. Trader Joe's scouts the world for new and inspiring foods and beverages. Only the ones that pass Trader Joe's employee taste tests make it to stores.

Just food, no preservatives. When you compare the labels on Trader Joe's products to items found at other stores, you'll notice something missing: a long list of chemicals, fillers, artificial flavors, and preservatives.

Nothing genetically engineered. Trader Joe's was among the first national grocers to remove genetically modified food from its private label products.

Actively "green." Trader Joe's has made all kinds of environmental "green lists" for its commitment to responsible sourcing of food. Trader Joe's brand eggs are cage-free. Hormone-free dairy products are the norm. Tuna is from "dolphin-safe" water (and as a result, low in mercury).

Wine and beer. In addition to great foods, Trader Joe's brings a wide and ever-evolving assortment of value-priced wines from all over the globe, including the famously nicknamed "Two Buck Chuck." Trader Joe's international beer selection is second to none.

Fun shopping experience. Balloons, hand-written chalkboard signs, lively music, and cheerful crewmembers decked in Hawaiian flair create a friendly and casual atmosphere.

So come on down to your nearest Trader Joe's with this cookbook in hand, and let us show you why this is our favorite grocer and our favorite way to cook.

Conversions and Rules of Thumb

Volume Measurements

3 teaspoons = 1 tablespoon

4 tablespoons = ¼ cup

16 tablespoons = 1 cup

2 cups = 1 pint

2 pints = 1 quart

4 quarts = 1 gallon

2 tablespoons = 1 fluid ounce

1 cup = 8 fluid ounces

Weight Measurements

16 ounces = 1 pound

Abbreviations

tsp = teaspoon

Tbsp = tablespoon

oz = ounce

lb = pound

pkg = package

Eyeballing Measurements

Most recipes don't require painstaking measurement unless you're baking. Ingredients can usually be eyeballed.

An easy way to eyeball cup measurements is to think of the volume of an average apple. That's about a cup. Half an apple, about half a cup. The volume of an egg is about ⅓ cup.

Pour a tablespoon of olive oil in your pan and see what it looks like in the pan. Once you get a feel for what it looks like, just eyeball it from then on.

Pour a teaspoon of salt in the palm of your hand. After you see that a few times, trust your eye as the judge.

A Few of our Favorite Things...

Condiments

Trader Joe's Sea Salt, Black Peppercorns, and Lemon Pepper with built-in grinder. Grinders make it a snap to have freshly ground salt and pepper on hand.

Two essential spices: If you have just two dry spices in your kitchen cabinet at home, we think they should be cinnamon and cumin, great for adding depth to entrées and desserts.

Fresh ginger. Peel it, bag it, and keep in the freezer. Grate as needed, but do not allow it to thaw completely before returning it to the freezer.

Frozen herbs. Trader Joe's carries frozen chopped garlic and herbs, conveniently packaged in little cubes that measure 1 clove or 1 tsp. They can be substituted for fresh ingredients in most recipes.

Parmesan cheese. It keeps for a long time in the fridge and is wonderful to have on hand for a variety of recipes.

Utensils

Lime squeezer. Roll and squeeze all you want—you can't get all the juice out of a lime or lemon quickly, efficiently, and cleanly without one of these. You'll be surprised at how easy it is to juice a lime or lemon with a lime squeezer. More importantly, it's impossible to be a Margarita master without owning one.

Binder clips. Don't bother with all those expensive clips to close your open bags of chips, cereal, or nuts. Nowadays, many bags have zipper locks, but if not, just grab a big box of office binder clips. They're cheap and do the job perfectly.

Silicone spoonula or spatula. These hardworking utensils are rated to 500° F, so they won't melt on a hot skillet. Great for stirring, flipping, and scraping all the good stuff out of a bowl or hot pan.

Kitchen shears. Scissors in the kitchen are underrated. Keep a dishwasher-safe pair handy for cutting up everything from herbs to sun dried tomatoes to cooked chicken.

Tongs. Handy for flipping chicken, tossing a salad, or mixing pasta and vegetables.

Cookware

Pizza stone. It should be at least ½ inch thick and always kept in the oven. Nice ones run between $30-40 and make all the difference in your pizza crust. Heat the oven to 500° F or above, and do not put dough on the stone until the oven and stone are fully heated. There's no other way to get pizza crust this good at home.

Seasoned cast iron skillet. To season, cover the pan with oil and bake in the oven at 250° F for 30 minutes. Then don't ever soap or scrub it again. Over time, baked-on oil will make the surface naturally nonstick. To wash, just soak in hot water and use a spatula to bump off any stubborn bits of food.

Basic necessities: A set of quality sharp knives, a good nonstick skillet, a few pots in different sizes, measuring spoons and cups, and a couple of baking dishes.

Appealing Appetizers

Spicy Tropical Shrimp Boats

All aboard! Shrimp, mango, and jalapeños set sail on endive boats. No utensils needed for this seafood adventure. The sweet flavors in the fruit salsa offset the slightly bitter taste of crunchy endive. Be prepared for the salsa's spicy kick!

1 cup frozen Medium Cooked Tail-Off Shrimp, thawed

½ cup Fire Roasted Papaya Mango Salsa

Salt and pepper

1 head fresh Belgian endive, leaves separated

2 Tbsp refrigerated Cilantro Dressing

Cilantro for garnish

1 Dice shrimp into cubes. Mix shrimp and salsa. Season with salt and pepper to taste.

2 Spoon shrimp mixture onto endive leaves. Arrange shrimp boats on serving platter and drizzle with dressing.

3 Garnish with cilantro.

Variation: For a more traditional (and less spicy) shrimp salad, omit salsa and instead mix ¼ cup Cilantro Dressing or other creamy dressing into the shrimp. Garnish with cilantro.

Prep time: 15 minutes
Serves 4 (2 boats each)

Per serving: 101 calories, 3 g fat, 0 g saturated fat, 14 g protein, 5 g carbs, 0 g fiber, 3 g sugar, 524 mg sodium

Macho Nacho

Our Macho Nacho is a casserole version of a nachos plate, with lots of crunch and flavor. It's a substantial dish with chili and fresh toppings, making it a nice quick dinner or an easy appetizer. Don't forget this recipe during game day!

---

8 oz corn tortilla chips (we used ½ of a 16-oz bag Organic White Corn Tortilla Chips)

1 (15-oz) can of your favorite chili (we like Organic Vegetarian Chili)

1 ½ cups Fancy Shredded Mexican Blend cheese

2 cups chopped tomato or quartered cherry tomatoes

1 cup (one tray) refrigerated Avocado's Number Guacamole

½ cup sour cream

½ cup Double Roasted Salsa or Chunky Salsa

¼ cup chopped fresh cilantro

1   Preheat oven to 375° F.

2   Scatter tortilla chips in a 9 x 13-inch baking pan and top with chili and cheese. Place pan in the oven for 10 minutes or until cheese is melted.

3   Take pan out of the oven and immediately add tomatoes, guacamole, and sour cream. Drizzle salsa over the top and sprinkle with cilantro. Serve immediately.

Prep and cooking time: 15-20 minutes
Serves 8

Per serving: 357 calories, 22 g fat, 6 g saturated fat, 10 g protein, 30 g carbs, 6 g fiber, 3 g sugar, 550 mg sodium

Apricot Baked Brie

When Deana was school age, her mom would order a prepared apricot Brie from the specialty grocery store in town, which only stocked it seasonally. She really didn't care for plain old Brie back then, but when she took that warm, apricot-covered melty concoction came out of the oven, she couldn't get enough. Even if you think you don't like Brie, try this baked version; you may not recognize it. This warm and creamy cheese dish is a great accompaniment to some grapes and a bottle of wine. One night, we had this dish with our Roasted Garlic (page 20) as appetizers and enjoyed it so much that we kept on eating and skipped dinner.

1 (~0.6 lb) wedge Brie cheese, such as Double Crème Brie

2 heaping Tbsp apricot preserves, such as Organic Reduced Sugar Apricot Preserves

1 handful raw sliced almonds

1 Tbsp Triple Sec (optional)

1 box water crackers

1 Preheat oven to 400° F.

2 Place the wedge of Brie in a small baking dish that is slightly bigger than the Brie. Top with apricot preserves, sprinkle on almonds, and drizzle Triple Sec over the top.

3 Cover tightly with foil and bake for 12-14 minutes or until cheese is melting. Remove from oven and serve with water crackers. Before your guests attack the Brie unrelentingly, remind them that the dish is hot.

Prep time: 5 minutes
Hands-off cooking time: 12-14 minutes
Serves 8

Per serving: 181 calories, 10 g fat, 6 g saturated fat, 9 g protein, 13 g carbs, 0 g fiber, 1 g sugar, 254 mg sodium

G Gluten Free   **V** Vegetarian

Use Savory Thins crackers

Roasted Garlic (Friends Be Damned)

Roasting mellows out garlic's strong flavor, and it becomes a creamy spread that you can eat on crackers or crusty bread. My 2- and 4-year-old eat it straight from the bulb. Pair with cheese, mix with mashed potatoes, or add to pasta dishes and steaks for great flavor. Garlic aids digestion and keeps your immune system peaked. Garlic also contains allicin, which reduces unhealthy fats and cholesterol in the system, one of the many reasons garlic is praised for its medicinal properties. Baking or roasting it whole (or eating it raw, of course, but that's between you and your friends) is the best way to preserve its properties.

Whole bulbs of garlic

1 Tbsp extra virgin olive oil per bulb

Freshly ground black pepper

1   Preheat oven to 400° F.

2   With a knife, cut tops off garlic bulbs, slicing across tips of cloves. Place each bulb on a square of aluminum foil, drizzle with olive oil, and sprinkle with pepper.

3   Wrap foil around each bulb and toss the wrapped bulbs in the oven (straight on the rack) for 30-40 minutes or until garlic cloves are completely soft and beginning to caramelize. (Just open the foil and take a peek.) For a large bulb (2.5 inches across), cooking time will be about 40 minutes.

4   When you gently press at the base of the clove, it will easily squeeze out whole.

Prep time: 5 minutes
Hands-off cooking time: 40 minutes
A large bulb serves 4

Per serving: 36 calories, 4 g fat, 1 g saturated fat, 0 g protein, 1 g carbs, 0 g fiber, 0 g sugar, 2 mg sodium

Wine Suggestion:

Try an off-dry Riesling or a sweet and crisp Sauvignon Blanc such as **Chateau Ste. Michelle Sauvignon Blanc,** fruity with enough acidic crispness and sweetness to balance the flavors of this dish.

Perfectly Peared Gorgonzola Quesadillas

Pears and Gorgonzola cheese are often paired in a salad — why not in a quesadilla? When grilled, the tortilla shells get crunchy on the outside with a warm soft cheese and fruit filling on the inside. Serve as an appetizer or as a dessert. You could make crepe versions instead of quesadillas.

4 medium-sized white flour tortillas, such as Organic Flour Tortillas

1 (8-oz) pkg Crumbled Gorgonzola Cheese

1 pear, thinly sliced (fresh or jarred)

1 Tbsp butter

1 cup Pear Sauce or applesauce

¼ cup Candied Walnuts or regular walnuts

1 Heat a skillet over medium heat.

2 While skillet is heating, assemble quesadillas. Sprinkle 2 Tbsp Crumbled Gorgonzola on one half of a tortilla. Place ¼ of the sliced pears over the cheese. Sprinkle another 2 Tbsp Gorgonzola on top of the pears. Fold tortilla in half, over the cheese and pear filling. Assemble remaining quesadillas.

3 Melt a dab of butter in the skillet and spread around. Grill quesadillas 1-2 minutes on each side, until tortillas are golden.

4 To serve, cut quesadillas in wedges and top with pear sauce and walnuts.

Prep and cooking time: *20 minutes*
Serves 8

Per half-quesadilla serving: 231 calories, 13 g fat, 7 g saturated fat, 9 g protein, 16 g carbs, 1 g fiber, 4 g sugar, 417 mg sodium

Use brown rice tortillas

Smokin' Salmon Crostini

This elegant appetizer takes just minutes to assemble. The crunchy toast offsets the creamy texture of the salmon and crème fraîche. Use wild Nova salmon if you can – it's less salty. Serve with your favorite cocktail.

24 pieces Sesame Melba Rounds

1 (4-oz) pkg Nova Smoked Wild Sockeye Salmon

¼ cup crème fraîche or sour cream

Chives, finely chopped, for garnish (or substitute green onions or dill)

1   Top each cracker with a piece of smoked salmon.

2   Add a dollop of crème fraîche and a sprinkle of chives.

Prep time: *10 minutes*
Serves 6

Per serving: 123 calories, 6 g fat, 3 g saturated fat, 6 g protein,
9 g carbs, 1 g fiber, 0 g sugar, 255 mg sodium

Deep Sea Adventure

Simple tail-on shrimp and cocktail sauce are that classic combination that everyone loves. Make it a tasty culinary adventure by taking it a step further with wasabi, garlic, Asian and salsa dipping sauces, all conveniently jarred. See if everyone can identify the unique flavors!

1 lb frozen Jumbo or Colossal Cooked Tail-On Shrimp, thawed

Try these dips:

Shrimp Cocktail Sauce

Wasabi Mayonnaise

Garlic Aioli Mustard Sauce or Hot & Sweet Mustard

General Tsao Stir Fry Sauce

Double Roasted Salsa

1 Fill 5 dipping bowls with each of the sauces.

2 Arrange shrimp around a platter and serve.

Prep time: 5 minutes
Serves 6

Per serving:
53 calories, 1 g fat,
0 g saturated fat,
12 g protein, 0 g carbs,
0 g fiber, 0 g sugar,
336 mg sodium

Gluten Free

Eggplant Tostada

This dish is similar to a Mexican tostada, a flat tortilla that is "toasted." The eggplant spread acts as a glue to keep toppings from falling off. Get creative with this dish and top it with any ingredients you have on hand, including seafood, chicken, or leftover vegetables.

4 medium-sized whole wheat flour tortillas

1 cup Eggplant Garlic Spread or Red Pepper Spread with Eggplant & Garlic

1 cup tomatoes, chopped

½ cup Crumbled Feta cheese

2 Tbsp chopped parsley

1   Preheat oven to 400° F.

2   Cover each tortilla with ¼ cup eggplant spread and place on baking sheet. Top with tomatoes and feta.

3   Bake for 10-12 minutes or until tortillas are golden and crisp on the edges.

4   Garnish with a sprinkle of parsley.

Variation: For a Mexican version, use Refried Black Bean Dip and top with tomatoes, corn, shredded cheddar cheese, and cilantro.

Prep time: *5 minutes*
Hands-off cooking time: *10- 12 minutes*
Serves 4

Per serving: 318 calories, 15 g fat, 3 g saturated fat,
6 g protein, 35 g carbs, 4 g fiber, 11 g sugar, 963 mg sodium

Gluten Free   Vegetarian
Use brown rice tortillas

Savory Vegan Pâté

Stop! Hold it right there! Put away all your preconceptions. Yes, it's vegan; yes, it's super healthy, and even more so since it's nearly raw; but it actually tastes good! It's like a nutty pilaf in a tasty sauce, with raisins and the crisp crunch of apples, perfect for a spread or a pita filling. Soaking the nuts makes them plump and soft and neutralizes the enzyme inhibitors, making the nuts easier to digest.

¾ cup raw whole cashews, soaked 8 hours or overnight (measure before soaking)

¾ cup raw whole almonds, soaked 8 hours or overnight (measure before soaking)

¼ cup raw sunflower seeds

1 Tbsp flax oil

¼ cup bagged Golden Roasted Flaxseed, Whole Seeds

1 ripe banana, peeled

2 Tbsp almond butter

2 Tbsp soy sauce

½ cup peeled and finely chopped Granny Smith apple

¼ cup raisins

1   After soaking, rinse nuts thoroughly and then drain.

2   Place nuts in a blender (or food processor) and pulse until they are well chopped (Don't blend so much that you turn it into nut butter). Pour in sunflower seeds, flax oil, and roasted flaxseeds. Pulse a few more times (or stir with a spoon) until combined.

3   In a medium bowl, mash banana with a fork. Add almond butter and soy sauce, stirring until it forms a sauce (don't worry about little lumps). Add nut mixture and stir until combined. Fold in apples and raisins.

4   Form a pâté with the mixture and serve with flatbread (such as Corn Tortilla Flat Breads shown in photo), crackers, or lavash; or stuff inside a pita with some greens.

Note: *Serve right away or that same day.*
Prep time: *20 minutes (not counting soaking time)*
Serves 8

Per serving: 318 calories, 24 g fat, 3 g saturated fat,
10 g protein, 21 g carbs, 5 g fiber, 8 g sugar, 228 mg sodium

Use tamari instead of soy sauce

Cooking with All Things Trader Joe's

Prosciutto-Wrapped Scallops

Prosciutto cooks up crisp in the oven and is a nice balance to the soft scallops. Serve these tasty morsels as an appetizer, or as an elegant dinner served on a bed of salad, couscous, or Orzo Pilaf (page 185).

---

1 lb jumbo scallops, thawed if frozen (about a dozen scallops)

6 slices Prosciutto, cut lengthwise in half, or bacon may be substituted

2 Tbsp Green Olive Tapenade or Mixed Olive Bruschetta

1 Preheat oven to 375° F.

2 Lightly pat scallops dry with a clean paper towel. Season scallops with the tapenade, making sure to coat all sides evenly.

3 Wrap each scallop with a band of prosciutto. Place seam side down in a buttered baking dish or cookie sheet. Spread scallops 2 inches apart so that they roast and don't steam.

4 Bake for 15-16 minutes. Do not overcook. Scallops are done when they are opaque and no longer translucent.

Variation: *For an Asian twist, flavor the scallops with General Tsao Stir Fry Sauce instead of tapenade.*

Prep time: *10 minutes*
Hands-off cooking time: *15-16 minutes*
Serves 4 *(about 3 scallops each)*

Per serving: 318 calories, 15 g fat, 3 g saturated fat, 6 g protein, 35 g carbs, 4 g fiber, 11 g sugar, 963 mg sodium

Polenta with Truffled Mushrooms

Ever wondered how to use truffle oil? In one word: drizzle. Drizzle over roasted vegetables, scrambled eggs, mashed potatoes, risotto, or pizza. Truffle oil will kick the flavors up a notch and take foods from fine to divine. Its woodsy, earthy flavor goes perfectly with mushrooms in this impressive but easy appetizer. You can brown the polenta slices in advance and warm the browned polenta in the microwave or under the broiler when you're ready to serve.

1 (18-oz) tube pre-cooked Organic Polenta, cut into ½-inch slices

2 Tbsp olive oil, divided

¼ tsp black pepper

2 cups sliced crimini mushrooms

½ tsp salt

2 tsp truffle oil, or substitute garlic infused olive oil for a milder flavor

¼ cup Freshly Shredded Parmesan Cheese or Crumbed Goat Cheese

Chopped chives (optional)

1   Heat a large nonstick skillet or grill pan over high heat.

2   Drizzle 1 Tbsp olive oil onto hot pan. Arrange polenta slices in pan in a single layer. Sprinkle with black pepper. Cook for 4 minutes on each side, or until lightly browned.

3   While polenta is cooking, heat remaining 1 Tbsp olive oil in a small pan. Cook mushrooms for 5 minutes, sprinkling in salt toward the end. Remove from heat. Drizzle with truffle oil and stir to combine.

4   Top each polenta round with a heaping spoonful of mushrooms and a sprinkle of cheese.

5   Garnish with chives.

Prep and cooking time: 20 minutes
Serves 4

Per serving: 212 calories, 13 g fat, 4 g saturated fat, 7 g protein, 19 g carbs, 1 g fiber, 2 g sugar, 716 mg sodium

Gluten Free   Vegetarian

Wine Suggestion:

Look for an earthy Pinot Noir.
Castle Rock Pinot Noir,
light and clean, has earthy
notes along with some cherry
and floral notes.

Breezy Caprese Salad

Fresh as spring, this is an informal version of the classic Italian salad. Colorful heirloom tomatoes are especially wonderful here, but any ripe tomatoes will do. Creamy fresh mozzarella is conveniently pre-sliced and ready when you are.

---

3 tomatoes, cut in thick slices

1 (8-oz) container Fresh Mozzarella Medallions, or slice your own

1 bunch basil leaves

2 Tbsp extra virgin olive oil

Pinch salt and pepper

1   Arrange tomato slices and cheese medallions on a simple platter. Tuck basil leaves between tomatoes and cheese.

2   Drizzle platter liberally with olive oil. Sprinkle generously with salt and pepper.

Prep time: 5 minutes
Serves 4

Per serving:
207 calories,
16 g fat,
6 g saturated fat,
13 g protein,
6 g carbs,
2 g fiber, 4 g sugar,
202 mg sodium

Herb Goat Cheese Log

How do you make fresh goat cheese go from simple to sublime, from plain to pretty? Roll a goat cheese log in fresh chopped herbs, nuts, and berries to complement its tangy taste and creamy texture. Serve with crackers, toasted baguette slices, or apple slices. Crumble leftovers on top of greens to make an extra special salad.

---

1 (8-oz) log Chevre goat cheese, plain (larger size is okay)

½ cup chopped and crushed Candied Pecans or regular pecans

½ cup chopped fresh basil

½ cup chopped dried cranberries

¼ tsp black pepper

1   Combine pecans, basil, cranberries, and pepper on a flat surface.

2   Unwrap goat cheese log and roll firmly in nut mixture, coating all surfaces.

Prep time: *5 minutes*
Serves 6

Per serving:
207 calories, 14 g fat,
6 g saturated fat,
8 g protein, 12 g carbs,
2 g fiber, 10 g sugar,
90 mg sodium

Sweet Potato Samosas

Samosas are traditionally deep-fried. Our version is heart-healthy and baked, but just as flavorful! We found the easy buttermilk crust recipe in the Moosewood Cookbook. Serve samosas with Cilantro Dressing or Sweet Chili Sauce.

Filling

1 (12-oz) bag Sweet Potato Spears or 1 (16-oz) bag cubed Yams

½ cup frozen peas

⅔ cup India Relish or spiced chutney

½ tsp salt

¼ cup fresh chopped cilantro

Buttermilk crust

2 ½ cups white flour

1 cup buttermilk or plain yogurt

½ tsp salt

1 Preheat oven to 400° F.

2 Combine sweet potatoes/yams and ½ cup water in a microwave-safe dish deep enough to mix in. Cover with a wet paper towel and microwave for 8 minutes or until tender.

3 While potatoes are cooking, prepare the crust. Mix flour, buttermilk, and salt with a fork until dough forms a ball. Dough will be quite soft. Divide dough into 10 egg-sized balls; roll each one out to a 6-inch circle on a floured surface.

4 Drain cooked potatoes and mash with a fork. Stir frozen peas into hot mashed potatoes – no need to defrost; they will thaw on their own. Stir in India Relish, salt, and cilantro. Mix well. Check seasonings; add relish if you prefer more spice.

5 Spoon ¼ cup of potato mixture into center of each crust. Fold dough around filling and seal edges by pressing crust firmly together. Make moon-shaped pies or more traditional triangular shapes (both shown in photo).

6 Place samosas on greased baking sheet. Bake for 20-25 minutes or until golden brown, flipping once if you want both sides browned evenly.

Prep time: 20 minutes
Hands-off cooking time: 20-25 minutes
Makes 10 samosas

Per samosa: 201 calories, 5 g fat, 0 g saturated fat, 5 g protein, 35 g carbs, 3 g fiber, 5 g sugar, 283 mg sodium

Wine Suggestion:

Spice for spice. Try Rocking Horse Zinfandel, soft on the tannins, for this vegetarian dish and a great value Zinfandel.

Italian Party Spread

Quick! You have 5 minutes to whip together an appetizer platter before guests arrive. It couldn't be easier to assemble a mouthwatering array of bruschettas, cheese, olives, and crusty breads. The great thing about this selection is that you can make it for 2 people or for 10 just as easily–simply eyeball the amounts. To make a casual evening of tasting and mingling, add our Apricot Baked Brie (page 19) and Roasted Garlic (page 20) to this spread along with a bottle of wine.

1 box water crackers

1 (8-oz) pkg Chevre goat cheese

1 container refrigerated Fresh Bruschetta Sauce

½ jar Mixed Olive Bruschetta

½ jar Sun Dried Tomato Bruschetta

1 container Ciliegine, Fresh Mozzarella balls

Rolled proscuitto slices

1 handful fresh basil leaves

½ jar pitted Kalamata olives

1 loaf warm Italian or French bread

Any hard cheese, such as Pecorino Romano, or Italian Truffle Cheese

1   To assemble goat cheese bruschettas, lay crackers in a single layer on a platter. Spread some goat cheese on each cracker and top with bruschetta sauce. They'll go fast!

2   Arrange all the other ingredients on a large tray or combination of bowls and platters. A crusty piece of bread topped with a basil leaf, some bruschetta, and cheese…perfection!

Prep time: 5 minutes
Serves up to 8

 Use Savory Thins crackers

 Omit prosciutto

Wine Suggestion:

For mature cheeses, olives, and bold flavors, try a big earthy wine, such as **Epicuro Nero d'Avola**. If serving sheep's milk cheeses, pair with Spanish **La Granja Tempranillo**.

Wine Suggestion:

Pair this flavorful spread with **Don Miguel Gascón Malbec,** an intense purple-red wine from Argentina, fruity and smooth.

Greek Party Spread

Like our Italian Party Spread, this is another festive party platter that can be made-to-order in just minutes. Bring home a taste of the Mediterranean and transport your guests to an exotic land of sun-bleached buildings set against bright blue waters. To make a complete but hassle-free dinner party, pick up a frozen Spinach Pie for dinner and prepared Baklava for dessert.

1 container refrigerated hummus (we like Mediterranean Hummus)

1 container refrigerated Tzatziki Dip or Cilantro & Chive Yogurt Dip

1 container refrigerated Dolmas (Stuffed Grape Leaves)

1 container refrigerated Greek Olive Medley

1 block Feta cheese

A selection of Pita bread wedges, Pita chips, Flatbread crackers, or water crackers

A selection of veggies to dip, such as bell peppers, baby carrots, celery sticks, cucumber slices, cherry tomatoes or quartered tomatoes

Bunch of grapes

Fresh mint leaves or basil leaves for garnish

1   Select a large platter. A wooden cutting block also works nicely.

2   Place hummus and tzatziki in bowls in the center. Arrange all other items around the dips, alternating colors.

3   Tuck bunches of mint or basil leaves into a few corners.

Prep time: *10 minutes*
Serves up to 8

G Gluten Free   **V** Vegetarian

Use Savory Thins crackers

Soups, Salads & Light Meals

Chicken Tortilla Soup

This warm, flavorful soup is sure to cure the common cold and the common soup. The best part is the contrast of fresh cilantro, fresh avocado, cheese, and crispy chips added at the last minute to this aromatic, spicy soup. It's *delicioso* - make extra!

4 boneless chicken thighs

3 cups chicken broth

2 cups water

1 yellow onion, quartered

1 tsp ground cumin

¾ cup Chunky Salsa

2 Tbsp lime juice (juice of 1 lime)

¼ cup chopped fresh cilantro

Toppings for each bowl

Handful of broken tortilla chips or strips

¼ cup Fancy Shredded Mexican Blend cheese

¼ of a ripe avocado, diced

1 Combine water, broth, and onion in a pot and bring to a boil. Add chicken, salsa, and cumin; boil until the chicken is poached, about 10 minutes.

2 Remove large onion pieces and discard. Using two forks, coarsely shred chicken and return to pot.

3 Add lime and simmer for an additional 5 minutes.

4 Remove pot from heat and add cilantro.

5 Ladle soup into individual bowls. Add broken tortilla chips, cheese, and avocado chunks to each bowl. Serve immediately.

Prep and cooking time: 20 minutes
Serves 4

Per serving: 383 calories, 25 g fat, 9 g saturated fat, 22 g protein, 20 g carbs, 5 g fiber, 7 g sugar, 977 mg sodium

 *Choose gluten free broth*

Antipasto Pasta Salad

This salad combines all the flavors of classic Italian antipasto. Use any combination of antipasto ingredients you have on hand. Because it can be served at room temperature, it is the perfect salad for picnics and large parties.

3 cups fusilli or Vegetable Radiatore (tri-color) pasta

1 cup salami or ham, sliced or cubed (cubed Applewood Smoked Cured Ham shown in photo)

1 (8-oz) container Marinated Mozzarella balls or 1 cup cubed Marinated Mozzarella braid

2 cups Oven Roasted Vegetables (page 186), diced into 1-inch pieces, or use ready-made jarred Roasted Red Peppers, Marinated Mushrooms, and refrigerated Fire Roasted Asparagus

½ cup pitted Kalamata olives

1 cup canned or frozen artichoke hearts, quartered

¼ cup Balsamic Vinaigrette or homemade White Wine Vinaigrette (see recipe below)

¼ cup fresh basil leaves, chopped

¼ cup grated Parmesan cheese

Salt and pepper to taste

1 Cook pasta according to package directions. Drain.

2 Mix all ingredients in a large bowl and toss well. Season with salt and pepper to taste.

White Wine Vinaigrette

1 ½ tsp white wine vinegar

1 ½ tsp fresh lemon juice

Generous pinch of salt

3 Tbsp extra virgin olive oil

1 Tbsp plain yogurt

Black pepper

1 Combine vinegar, lemon juice, and salt. Pour in olive oil and whisk until combined. Stir in yogurt and black pepper to taste.

Prep and cooking time: 15 minutes
Hands-off cooking time: 10 minutes
Serves 8

Per serving: 392 calories, 26 g fat, 8 g saturated fat, 15 g protein, 24 g carbs, 2 g fiber, 2 g sugar, 996 mg sodium

 Use brown rice pasta

 Omit salami/ham

Stuffed Red Peppers

Stuffed bell peppers are a delicious gourmet side or vegetarian main dish, but the stuffing is typically complex and time-consuming. We kept the complex taste but got rid of the long prep time. We have two versions: one with flavorful croutons & tomatoes and one with a pine nut & mushroom risotto, and they're both easy!

2 large red bell peppers, halved lengthwise with seeds and pith removed

1 ½ cups chopped tomatoes (~3 Roma tomatoes)

1 ½ cups (half a bag) Parmesan Crisps or Cheese & Garlic Croutons, coarsely crushed

¾ cup refrigerated Fresh Bruschetta Sauce

⅔ cup Shredded 3 Cheese Blend

1　Preheat oven to 350° F.

2　Place pepper halves on oiled baking dish. Mix together tomato, crushed crisps, bruschetta, and cheese. Stuff this mixture inside pepper halves, compacting lightly.

3　Bake uncovered for 30-35 minutes or until cheese is melted and top is golden.

Prep time: *10 minutes*
Hands-off cooking time: *30-35 minutes*
Makes 4 stuffed pepper halves

Per stuffed pepper half: 190 calories, 10 g fat, 3 g saturated fat, 8 g protein, 18 g carbs, 3 g fiber, 8 g sugar, 397 mg sodium

Stuffing Variation

1 bag frozen Mushroom Risotto or Asparagus Risotto, about 2 cups cooked

½ cup toasted pine nuts

⅔ cup shredded or sliced mozzarella cheese

1　Prepare risotto according to package instructions. Mix in pine nuts.

2　Stuff red peppers with this mixture and top with cheese.

3　Bake as before.

Per serving: 295 calories, 21 g fat, 6 g saturated fat, 10 g protein, 19 g carbs, 2 g fiber, 6 g sugar, 236 mg sodium

Italian Wedding Soup

Despite common belief, the name for this soup actually has nothing to do with a couple's big day. It refers to the winning combination of greens and meat. In Italian, two things that go well together are said to be "well married," and hence the name for this tasty dish. There are endless variations to wedding soup; just make sure meat and greens are involved.

20 frozen Party Size Mini Meatballs, about half a package, or use 1 bag frozen Turkey Meatballs, Italian Style Meatballs, or Meatless Meatballs

1 Tbsp extra virgin olive oil

1 small onion, chopped, or 1 cup bagged Freshly Diced Onions

1 clove garlic, crushed, or 1 cube frozen Crushed Garlic

½ cup diced carrots or halved baby carrots

4 cups (one 32-oz carton) low-sodium chicken or vegetable broth

3 cups Swiss chard or spinach (if using frozen spinach, use only 1 cup)

¼ cup chopped fresh parsley

¼ cup grated or shredded Parmesan cheese

1   Heat olive oil over medium-high heat. Add onions, garlic, and carrots. Cook for 5 minutes.

2   Add chicken broth and meatballs. Bring mixture to a boil. Reduce heat and simmer for 20 minutes. Add Swiss chard and boil for 5 minutes longer.

3   Ladle into soup bowls. Garnish with parsley and Parmesan cheese.

Prep time: 15 minutes
Hands-off cooking time: 20 minutes
Serves 6

Per serving: 179 calories, 11 g fat, 4 g saturated fat,
11 g protein, 8 g carbs, 1 g fiber, 2 g sugar, 402 mg sodium

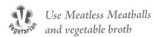 *Use Meatless Meatballs and vegetable broth*

Hearts and Snaps Salad

Hearts of palm are great straight out of the can and are high in iron and vitamins (and low in calories, for those who are counting). Combine them with sweet snap peas, refreshing cucumber, ripe tomatoes, tangy feta, and fresh parsley for a cool and quick salad. This crispy, fresh dish can be used as a colorful starter salad or light side dish. A splash of creamy dressing brings it all together.

1 cup sliced hearts of palm (about 3 sticks), available canned or fresh

1 cup chopped cucumbers (about 2 Persian cucumbers or 1 medium cucumber)

1 cup halved or quartered cherry/cocktail tomatoes

1 cup sugar snap peas, chopped in thirds

¼ cup chopped parsley (cilantro may be substituted)

¼ cup Crumbled Feta

¼ cup Goddess Dressing

1 Combine vegetables, cheese, and parsley in a bowl.

2 Toss with dressing.

Prep time: *10 minutes*
Serves 4

*Per serving: 138 calories,
9 g fat, 1 g saturated fat,
5 g protein, 10 g carbs,
3 g fiber, 5 g sugar,
276 mg sodium*

Mediterranean Lentil Salad

Tender pre-cooked lentils make this salad a mix-and-serve breeze. With a light, lemony, fresh taste, this lentil salad is a great side dish or light lunch. Serve with our Olive-Stuffed Bread (page 177). If you have leftovers, improvise a little and use them in our Vegetarian Hummus and Lentil Wrap (page 147).

1 (17.6-oz) pkg refrigerated Steamed Lentils (about 2 ½ cups)

1 ½ cups chopped tomato (we like to use cocktail tomatoes or baby Romas in this recipe)

½ cup chopped fresh parsley

1 Tbsp fresh mint (optional)

1 Tbsp lemon juice

2 Tbsp extra virgin olive oill

1   Combine lentils, tomatoes, parsley, and mint.

2   Whisk together lemon juice and olive oil. Pour dressing over salad, stirring gently to combine.

Prep time: *5 minutes*
Serves 6

Per serving:
227 calories, 7 g fat,
1 g saturated fat,
14 g protein,
29 g carbs, 11 g fiber,
4 g sugar,
308 mg sodium

Peanutty Sesame Noodles

These are the fresh and tasty sesame peanut noodles you remember from your favorite Chinese restaurant. Serve these flavorful noodles at room temperature or cold right out of the fridge. Add cooked chicken or tofu chunks to make it a standalone one-dish meal. Or pair with Soyaki Broiled Salmon (page 151).

8 oz (half a package) spaghetti noodles

Easy Peanutty Sauce (recipe below)

1 cup shredded carrot, available pre-shredded in the produce section

1 cup sliced cucumber

2 green onions, chopped

¼ cup roasted peanuts, crushed

1 Cook noodles according to package directions. Drain.

2 Pour Easy Peanutty Sauce over noodles and toss until noodles are evenly coated. Add carrots and cucumber. Toss gently.

3 Top with green onions and crushed peanuts.

Easy Peanutty Sauce

¼ cup Soyaki or Veri Veri Teriyaki

¼ cup creamy salted peanut butter

2 Tbsp toasted sesame oil

¼ cup water

1 Whisk Soyaki, peanut butter, and sesame oil until blended.

2 Add water and mix well.

Prep time: *10 minutes*
Hands-off cooking time: *10 minutes*
Serves 6

Per serving: 463 calories, 22 g fat, 3 g saturated fat, 15 g protein, 55 g carbs, 8 g fiber, 9 g sugar, 526 mg sodium

Asian Dumpling Soup

Here is our version of wonton soup using Asian steam-fried dumplings. In Japan, the dumplings are called gyozas, and in China, they are called *guo tie* (literally meaning "pot stick"), commonly known as potstickers. Most people are familiar with the pan-fried appetizer version, but the dumplings also work really well in soups. Adding a beaten egg at the end creates delicate ribbons reminiscent of egg drop soup. You can easily create a vegetarian version of this soup using vegetable gyozas and broth.

1 (16-oz) bag frozen gyoza

4 cups (one 32-oz carton) low-sodium chicken or vegetable broth

1 tsp soy sauce

1 clove garlic, crushed, or 1 cube frozen Crushed Garlic

3 cups refrigerated Stir Fry Vegetables, any variety, or frozen Stir-Fry Vegetables

1 egg (optional)

1 tsp toasted sesame oil

Black pepper to taste

1 In a medium pot, heat broth, soy sauce, and garlic over medium-high heat. Bring mixture to a boil. Add gyoza and vegetables. When mixture boils again, reduce heat to medium-low and cook for 5 minutes.

2 If using egg, beat with a fork until frothy. Slowly pour into boiling soup in a thin stream, creating cooked ribbons of egg. If you prefer, you can pan-fry the egg and cut into strips or squares. Use as a garnish.

3 Remove from heat. Stir in sesame oil. Sprinkle with black pepper to taste.

Prep and cooking time: 15 minutes
Serves 4

Per serving: 234 calories, 4 g fat, 1 g saturated fat, 10 g protein, 36 g carbs, 6 g fiber, 10 g sugar, 773 mg sodium

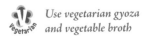 *Use vegetarian gyoza and vegetable broth*

Cooking with All Things Trader Joe's

Creamy Lemony Linguine

Linguine, flavored with mushrooms and a zingy lemon pepper cream sauce, is a nice side dish for chicken or meat, or can even be a main entrée in itself. Serve with a green salad or Caesar salad. This recipe doesn't rely on seasonal ingredients and is a snap to make. The Trader Joe's Lemon Pepper seasoning gives it a tasty kick without being overpowering. We can't guarantee good results using other brands of lemon pepper seasoning, which may have peculiar aftertastes according to one of our testers.

1 (16-oz) box or bag linguine pasta

1 cup heavy cream or whipping cream

½ cup Freshly Shredded Parmesan Cheese

Juice of 1 lemon (2 Tbsp)

2 tsp Lemon Pepper (in a grinder container)

2 Tbsp butter, unsalted

1 (10-oz) container sliced white mushrooms

1   Prepare linguine according to package instructions.

2   While linguine cooks, prepare the sauce. In a small saucepan over medium heat, pour in heavy cream and add Parmesan, stirring until Parmesan is melted into the cream. Stir in lemon juice and lemon pepper. Turn heat to lowest setting while you prepare the mushrooms.

3   In a hot skillet, melt butter and add mushrooms. Cook for 1 minute, stirring constantly, and take off heat before mushrooms give off any water. You want to keep mushrooms plump and firm, not stewed and shrunken.

4   Drain pasta when done and place in a large bowl. Pour sauce over pasta, add mushrooms, and toss together until sauce is evenly distributed.

5   Top with more Parmesan and serve.

Prep and cooking time: *15-20 minutes*
Serves 8

Per serving: 370 calories, 16 g fat, 10 g saturated fat, 12 g protein, 46 g carbs, 3 g fiber, 4 g sugar, 153 mg sodium

Use brown rice pasta

Warm Goat Cheese Salad

Goat cheese rounds are heated just enough to create a crusty layer without melting the cheese. This restaurant favorite is easy to make at home, especially with pre-sliced goat cheese medallions. We use almond meal instead of traditional breadcrumbs, both for flavor and nutritional value.

---

1 (5.4-oz) pkg Chevre Medallions or 1 (8-oz) log Chevre goat cheese, sliced

1 egg white, beaten

½ cup Just Almond Meal or breadcrumbs

2 Tbsp olive oil

1 (5-oz) bag Organics Baby Spring Mix salad

⅓ cup refrigerated Champagne Pear Vinaigrette or homemade Orange Champagne Vinaigrette (double the recipe on page 80)

1 Dip each goat cheese round in egg white and then coat in almond meal. If you're prepping ahead of time, place breaded goat cheese rounds in refrigerator until ready to cook. Cheese rounds should be cold and firm so they don't melt when fried.

2 Heat olive oil in a nonstick pan over medium heat. Fry cheese rounds for 1 minute on each side or until browned. Promptly remove from heat before cheese melts.

3 Pour vinaigrette over salad mix and toss until coated. Place warm cheese on dressed salad and serve immediately.

Tip: If you're slicing a goat cheese log yourself, don't use a knife or you'll end up with a gooey mess. Using unflavored dental floss, hold both ends tightly and press taut floss down through goat cheese.

Prep and cooking time: *20 minutes*
Serves 4

Per serving: 392 calories, 29 g fat, 15 g saturated fat, 20 g protein, 13 g carbs, 1 g fiber, 5 g sugar, 376 mg sodium

Use almond meal instead of breadcrumbs

Black Bean and Ricotta-Stuffed Portabellas

Everyone that first sees this recipe thinks, "Black beans and ricotta…are you sure?" but then follows up with, "Wow, it really works!" We wouldn't steer you wrong. The fillings have lots of complementary flavors and textures, and the portabellas are a hearty and substantial base. This tasty recipe can really do triple duty as an appetizer, a side dish, or a light dinner.

2 large portabella mushroom caps

½ cup ricotta cheese

½ cup canned black beans

2 Tbsp refrigerated Fresh Bruschetta Sauce

½ cup Shredded Mozzarella Cheese

1   Preheat oven to 400° F.

2   Don't wash the portabellas. Instead use a mushroom brush or a clean kitchen towel to wipe the caps.

3   Cut stems completely off the portabella caps, and place caps upside down on an oiled baking sheet or pan. Combine ricotta and black beans. Spread this mixture inside the caps. Do not overfill since caps will shrink slightly as they cook. Add 1 Tbsp bruschetta sauce on top of the filling and top each cap with mozzarella.

4   Bake for 12-14 minutes. Do not overcook or the portabellas will cook down and get very watery. Serve immediately.

Tip: Depending on the size of your portabellas, you may have leftover filling. Don't toss it. The next morning, fill a tortilla with the mixture and some bruschetta and take it along for lunch. Use the leftover bruschetta and some goat cheese to top some crackers (Italian Party Spread, page 38).

Prep time: *5 minutes*
Hands-off cooking time: *12-14 minutes*
Serves 2

Per serving: 341 calories, 16 g fat, 11 g saturated fat, 27 g protein, 18 g carbs, 5 g fiber, 3 g sugar, 434 mg sodium

Tortellini and Chicken Sausage Soup

This hearty soup is a leaner version of one that was demonstrated at a local Trader Joe's store. You would never guess this home cooked flavor took only minutes to make. Omit the chicken sausage for a vegetarian version.

1 cup dry Tortellini with Mixed Cheese Filling (any flavor dried tortellini is fine)

2 pre-cooked Mushroom Asiago Gourmet Chicken Sausages, cut into ½-inch slices (or other variety – there's plenty to choose from)

1 (14.5-oz) can Fire Roasted Whole Tomatoes, including juices, or regular canned tomatoes can be substituted though they are not as flavorful

1 (28-oz) can Rich Onion Soup, or use 1 (32-oz) carton chicken broth and only 1 cup water

2 cups water

2 cups frozen Greens with Envy, or other greens such as frozen spinach or green beans

Grated or shredded Parmesan cheese

1   Cut tomatoes into bite-size pieces. Mix tomatoes (including juices), onion soup, and water in a large pot. Bring to a boil.

2   Add tortellini, sausage, and greens. When mixture comes to a boil again, cover, reduce heat to low, and simmer for 17 minutes.

3   Sprinkle generously with Parmesan cheese and serve immediately.

Prep time: *5 minutes*
Hands-off cooking time: *20 minutes*
Serves 6

Per serving: 217 calories, 6 g fat, 1 g saturated fat, 10 g protein, 23 g carbs, 4 g fiber, 5 g sugar, 934 mg sodium

Persian Green Bean Rice

Here's a moist, flavorful rice dish with colorful tomatoes and green beans, brought together with the aromatic combination of cinnamon, saffron, and garlic. You can add frozen Turkey Meatballs to the pot when you layer the ingredients and create an easy one-pot dinner.

2 cups uncooked basmati rice

1 tsp salt

2 Tbsp butter

2 Tbsp extra virgin olive oil, divided

1 lb (3 cups) green beans, washed and cut to ½-1 inch lengths

1 clove garlic, crushed, or 1 cube frozen Crushed Garlic

1 (14.5-oz) can Fire Roasted Whole Tomatoes, diced, half drained, or plain canned diced tomatoes are also okay, half drained

1 tsp cinnamon

½ tsp Spanish Saffron

1 Place saffron in a small cup; add 1 Tbsp hot water and stir. Set aside.

2 Rinse rice and drain. Place rice in a large pot, fill with 8 cups water and salt; heat to boiling. Boil for 4 minutes. Rice should be tender to the bite but not fully cooked. Drain in a colander.

3 While rice is cooking, add 1 Tbsp olive oil to a large skillet and add green beans, garlic, diced tomatoes, and cinnamon. Stir lightly until combined. Cover and cook for 10 minutes.

4 Put 1 Tbsp butter and 1 Tbsp olive oil in the pot you used for the rice, and place it on medium heat. When the butter is melted, put ¼ of the rice on the bottom, then ⅓ of the green bean mixture. Continue alternating layers, forming a mound shape. Pour saffron water over the top and dot with remaining butter. Cover pot, reduce heat to low, and steam for 45 minutes.

Prep and cooking time: *15 minutes*
Hands-off cooking time: *45 minutes*
Serves 6

Per serving: 339 calories, 9 g fat, 3 g saturated fat, 7 g protein, 58 g carbs, 3 g fiber, 4 g sugar, 339 mg sodium

Asian Shrimp and Noodle Soup

Noodle soup is a staple in Asian countries, made with a myriad of different noodles. You can substitute any noodles you like, even spaghetti! Our recipe makes an easy and light noodle soup, with rich flavors of ginger and wild mushrooms. For a Japanese twist, try prepared Tempura Shrimp or Tempura Vegetables (both available frozen) instead of regular cooked shrimp; top the soup with tempura just before serving.

---

4 cups (one 32-oz carton) low sodium chicken broth

1 cup water

1 Tbsp soy sauce

1 tsp crushed ginger

One small bundle (¾-inch diameter) Brown Rice Spaghetti Pasta or Rice Sticks

½ cup (⅔ bag) dried Mixed Wild Mushrooms, rinsed (don't bother hydrating)

½ tsp freshly ground black pepper

1 cup frozen Medium or Large Cooked Tail-Off Shrimp

1 cup bagged Stir Fry Vegetables, Napa Cabbage variety, or 1 cup shredded white cabbage and bok choy

1 Tbsp toasted sesame oil

1 Add the broth, water, soy sauce, and ginger to a medium pot, bringing to a boil.

2 Add noodles, mushrooms, and black pepper. Bring to a boil again and cook for 6 minutes.

3 Add frozen shrimp, vegetables, and sesame oil. Bring to a boil again and cook for an additional 3-4 minutes or until pasta is *al dente*, skimming the top if necessary.

Prep and cooking time: *15 minutes*
Serves 4

Per serving: 209 calories, 7 g fat, 1 g saturated fat, 36 g protein, 28 g carbs, 3 g fiber, 6 g sugar, 608 mg sodium

Life is a Bowl of Cherries, Pine Nuts, and Spinach Salad

The creation of this salad was a complete accident. I was at a potluck pottery workshop where I tried a tasty salad and asked the lady for the recipe. When I met her again, I thanked her for the recipe and told her that the pine nuts, cherries and feta were amazing with the spinach. She laughed and told me that her salad recipe was arugula with blue cheese, walnuts, and apples. So much for my memory…I still need to try her version.

Montmorency cherries are the most popular sour cherry in the U.S and they give a great sweet/tart balance to the feta and pine nuts in this spinach salad. This salad is high in antioxidants from the cherries and in folic acid from the spinach (highest when raw).

---

1 (6-oz) bag baby spinach

½ cup Crumbled Feta cheese

½ cup dried Tart Montmorency Cherries

½ cup toasted pine nuts

6 Tbsp Balsamic Vinaigrette, or make your own (recipe below)

1   Combine ingredients, toss, and serve immediately.

2   The salad can be assembled ahead of time, but don't add the vinaigrette until you're ready to serve, or the spinach will wilt down.

Prep time: *5 minutes*
Serves 4

Homemade Balsamic Vinaigrette

4 Tbsp extra virgin olive oil

2 Tbsp balsamic vinegar

¼ tsp dried basil

¼ tsp Dijon mustard

¼ tsp honey or a pinch of sugar

1   Whisk together vinaigrette ingredients.

2   Vinaigrette keeps for a few days in a closed container, such as a glass jar with a lid.

Per serving: 249 calories, 22 g fat, 4 g saturated fat, 3 g protein, 14 g carbs, 2 g fiber, 9 g sugar, 151 mg sodium

Le French Lentil Soup

The best, most delicate lentils are French lentils, but they take longer to cook than other varieties. Thanks to pre-cooked lentils imported from France, this earthy soup can be made in minutes instead of hours. This recipe has fooled guests who staunchly claimed to dislike lentils, so test it on your own lentil-phobe. Ham or sausage makes this soup a hearty meal, but you can leave out the meat out for a vegetarian version.

1 (17.6-oz) pkg refrigerated Steamed Lentils (about 2 ½ cups)

2 Tbsp olive oil

1 large onion, chopped, or 2 cups bagged Freshly Diced Onions

1 cup sliced carrots

1 tsp ground cumin

4 cups (one 32-oz carton) low-sodium chicken or vegetable broth

1 cup diced Applewood Smoked Cured Ham (optional)

1 Tbsp fresh lemon juice

Salt and pepper to taste

2 Tbsp chopped cilantro

Sour cream (optional)

1 Heat olive oil in a large saucepan over medium-high heat.

2 Cook onions and carrots for 10 minutes or until onions soften. Stir in cumin and salt; cook for 1 minute longer to toast cumin.

3 Add chicken broth, lentils, and ham. Bring to a boil for a minute to heat everything through.

4 Remove from heat and stir in lemon juice. Add salt and pepper to taste.

5 Garnish with sour cream and cilantro.

Prep and cooking time: *20 minutes*
Serves 6

Per serving: 204 calories, 7 g fat, 1 g saturated fat, 14 g protein, 22 g carbs, 7 g fiber, 4 g sugar, 554 mg sodium

 Choose gluten-free broth

 Omit ham and use vegetable broth

Pasta alla Checca

This style of pasta is a favorite all over Italy in the summer, when tomatoes and basil are at their peak. You don't have to cook a thing except for the pasta. Lovers of fresh sauces on pasta, rejoice! The mozzarella cheese will soften slightly with the heat of the pasta, making for chewy cheese balls dotted throughout the pasta.

---

8 oz (half a package) linguine or spaghetti pasta

1 (8-oz) container refrigerated Fresh Bruschetta Sauce

¼ cup grated Parmesan cheese

1 (8-oz) container Ciliegine, Fresh Mozzarella balls

¼ cup chopped basil

1   Cook pasta in salted water according to package directions. Drain.

2   Add bruschetta and Parmesan cheese. Mix well to coat pasta evenly.

3   Stir in mozzarella balls gently, being careful not to break them. Top with basil and serve immediately.

Prep time: *5 minutes*
Hands-off cooking time: *10 minutes*
Serves 4

Per serving: 421 calories, 19 g fat, 7 g saturated fat, 22 g protein, 46 g carbs, 2 g fiber, 7 g sugar, 430 mg sodium

Black Bean Soup

One of our favorites. This soup is a hearty, spicy soup with the warm earthy flavor of cumin and the zing of fresh lime. We like it with tortilla chips on the side. It makes a great meal by itself, or it can be paired with one of our quesadilla recipes for a bigger meal. Not only are black beans high in fiber and folate, but they rival grapes and cranberries for their antioxidant properties. Sensitive to sulfites? Black beans contain the trace mineral molybdenum, which counteracts sulfites. So uncork that bottle of red later tonight.

1 medium yellow onion, peeled and chopped, or 1 ½ cups bagged Freshly Diced Onions

1 clove garlic, crushed, or 1 cube frozen Crushed Garlic

2 Tbsp extra virgin olive oil

1 tsp ground cumin

2 (15-oz) cans black beans (do not drain)

1 cup (half a jar) Chunky Salsa

2 Tbsp lime juice (juice of 1 lime)

Plain yogurt, such as Plain Cream Line Yogurt, or sour cream (optional)

1 In a medium pot, sauté onions in olive oil until they are soft and translucent.

2 Sprinkle in cumin and garlic and sauté for a minute; pour in black beans (including juices), salsa, and lime. Stir to combine and bring to a simmer. Simmer covered for 20 minutes.

3 Ladle soup into individual bowls and top with a dollop of yogurt.

Prep time: 10 minutes
Hands-off cooking time: 20 minutes
Serves 5

Per serving: 234 calories, 6 g fat, 1 g saturated fat, 9 g protein, 35 g carbs, 9 g fiber, 7 g sugar, 879 mg sodium

Zesty Shrimp and Scallops on Greens

The subtle sweet and spicy tones of the Pineapple Salsa and the fresh flavor of cilantro are tasty additions to shrimp and scallops. You can serve this dish as an impressive little starter salad or increase the portions for a healthy entrée. If you haven't discovered Trader Joe's Cilantro Dressing yet, you may be about to meet your favorite dressing.

Salad

½ (5-oz) bag Organics Baby Spring Mix

2 Tbsp refrigerated Cilantro Dressing

12 spears of fresh asparagus, cut into thirds

2 Tbsp extra virgin olive oil, divided

Salt and pepper to taste

Seafood

1 cup (½ lb or ½ bag) frozen Medium or Large Cooked Tail-Off Shrimp, thawed

1 cup (½ lb or ½ bag) frozen small or medium scallops, thawed and pat dry

½ cup Pineapple Salsa

1 Tbsp chopped fresh cilantro

1   Preheat oven to 400° F, if using fresh asparagus.

2   If using fresh asparagus, toss and coat asparagus in 1 Tbsp olive oil, season with salt and pepper, and bake for 10-15 minutes, depending on size of stalks.

3   While asparagus is roasting, sauté scallops in 1 Tbsp olive oil for 3-5 minutes or until opaque, adding shrimp at the very end. If using raw shrimp, cook them with the scallops. Add salsa and sauté for additional minute.

4   Toss spring greens with dressing and divide it among serving plates. Top with asparagus and seafood mixture, and garnish generously with cilantro.

Prep and cooking time: *15-20 minutes*
Serves 2 as an entrée

Per serving: 382 calories, 18 g fat, 3 g saturated fat, 45 g protein, 10 g carbs, 1 g fiber, 5 g sugar, 653 mg sodium

Can't Beet It Mandarin Orange Salad

This colorful salad combines the fresh flavors and colors of fall. Forget the days of cooking and peeling your own beets – and say goodbye to clothes stained with beet juice. Fully prepared beets are at your beck and call in the produce section. To save time, we use canned Mandarin oranges, but fresh orange, grapefruit, or Clementine tangerine segments would also be good.

---

1 (8-oz) pkg refrigerated Steamed & Peeled Baby Beets (about 5 small beets)

3 Tbsp refrigerated Champagne Pear Vinaigrette or Homemade Orange Champagne Vinaigrette (recipe below)

1 (11-oz) can Mandarin oranges, drained

1 Tbsp chopped fresh mint or basil

1 Tbsp Crumbled Goat Cheese

1   Cut beets into quarters. Pour vinaigrette over beets and stir.

2   Add orange segments and toss very gently; the orange segments are fragile.

3   Sprinkle mint and goat cheese crumbles on top.

Homemade Orange Champagne Vinaigrette

½ tsp Hot & Sweet Mustard, or ¼ tsp mustard + ¼ tsp honey

1 Tbsp Orange Muscat Champagne Vinegar

2 Tbsp extra virgin olive oil

Generous pinch of salt

1   Whisk all ingredients together until dressing becomes a creamy emulsion.

Prep time: *10 minutes*
Serves 4

Per serving: 146 calories, 8 g fat, 1 g saturated fat, 1 g protein, 18 g carbs, 1 g fiber, 16 g sugar, 114 mg sodium

Pesto Gazpacho

Our twist on the traditional gazpacho, paying homage to the Italian flavors of pine nuts and fresh basil.   We like the flavor of raw pine nuts in this recipe, but if the taste is too "piney" for you, stick with toasted pine nuts. This soup is great at room temperature!

4 cups (one 32-oz carton) Organic Creamy Tomato Soup

2 Tbsp fresh basil

½ cup raw pine nuts

1   Combine all ingredients in a blender, saving a bit of basil and pine nuts for garnish.

2   Pureé until smooth. Serve topped with basil and pine nuts.

Prep time: *10 minutes*
Serves 4

Per serving:
205 calories,
12 g fat,
2 g saturated fat,
8 g protein,
17 g carbs, 2 g fiber,
11 g sugar,
750 mg sodium

Notcho Ordinary Gazpacho

Our take on the famous cold Andalusian soup, fresh with the cooling aroma and taste of cucumber and cilantro. A light and refreshing soup for a summer meal served on the patio. Don't forget the sangria!

---

4 cups (one 32-oz carton) Organic Creamy Tomato Soup

2 cups peeled and coarsely chopped cucumber (2 medium-sized cucumbers)

3 Tbsp lime juice (juice of 2 limes)

1 green bell pepper, stems and seeds removed

1 cup Soup & Oyster Crackers

1 cup Chunky Salsa

2 Tbsp cilantro

1 Combine all ingredients in a blender, saving a bit of cilantro or a few cucumber slices for garnish.

2 Pureé until smooth. Chill and serve cold.

Prep time: *15 minutes*
Serves 4

Per serving:
160 calories,
6 g fat,
2 g saturated fat,
2 g protein,
26 g carbs, 3 g fiber,
6 g sugar,
42 mg sodium

Main Meals

Wine Suggestion:

Pick a fruity Chardonnay like **Bogle Chardonnay**, a full-bodied wine with apple and pineapple flavors and enough acidity to balance out the salsa. Another great pick is **Trader Joe's Coastal Chardonnay**, a smooth and fruity wine that can stand up to this flavorful dish.

Go Go Mango Chicken

Chicken is the perfect medium for a great-tasting topping; in fact, it's a little boring without it! This recipe is a favorite of adults and kids alike. Mildly spicy salsa and sweet mango chunks form a flavorful, tropically inspired partnership. Serve with Cilantro Jasmine Rice (recipe below) or a side of steamed vegetables.

---

2 skinless, boneless chicken breasts

1 (12-oz) jar Pineapple Salsa

1 ½ cups frozen Mango Chunks or frozen Tropical Fruit Trio

1 Preheat oven to 350° F.

2 Place chicken breasts in a baking dish, cover with salsa, and top with mango chunks (don't bother thawing). Lightly drape with aluminum foil.

3 Bake for 30-40 minutes or until chicken is done and juices run clear when cut. Be careful not to overcook.

Prep time: *5 minutes*
Hands-off cooking time: *30-40 minutes*
Serves 4
Per serving (½ breast): 181 calories, 2 g fat, 0 g saturated fat, 14 g protein, 13 g carbs, 1 g fiber, 5 g sugar, 380 mg sodium

Cilantro Jasmine Rice

1 cup uncooked jasmine rice

2 cups water

½ tsp salt

¼ cup finely chopped fresh cilantro

1 Bring water to a boil. Add salt and rice. Cover, reduce heat to medium-low, and steam for 20 minutes or until water is absorbed.

2 Stir in cilantro.

Prep time: *5 minutes*
Hands-off cooking time: *20 minutes*
Serves 4
Per serving: 180 calories, 1 g fat, 0 g saturated fat, 3 g protein, 40 g carbs, 1 g fiber, 0 g sugar, 291 mg sodium

Pizza Bianca with Prosciutto and Asparagus

In Rome, traditional pizza Bianca or "white pizza" is made with a simple selection of mozzarella cheese, olive oil, and herbs. It is often eaten for breakfast. We've added colorful toppings to make a heartier pizza that's great any time of day. You won't miss the tomato sauce in this flavor-packed white pizza.

1 (1-lb) bag refrigerated Ready to Bake Pizza Dough or Garlic & Herb Dough

1 tsp extra virgin olive oil

1 cup Quattro Formaggio shredded cheese

4 slices prosciutto, cut into 2- or 3-inch pieces

½ cup fresh or frozen asparagus spears, thawed, and cut diagonally into 3-inch pieces

2 Tbsp Shaved Parmigiano Reggiano (Parmesan) cheese

¼ cup toasted pine nuts

¼ tsp black pepper

1   Preheat oven to 500° F, preferably with a pizza stone inside.

2   Roll dough into a 10-inch circle on a lightly floured surface. Drizzle oil and rub evenly all over dough.

3   Sprinkle shredded cheese onto dough. Arrange prosciutto and asparagus pieces evenly over dough. Top with Parmesan cheese, pine nuts, and black pepper.

4   Transfer to pizza stone or baking sheet. Bake for 10 minutes or until crust is golden. Let sit for 5 minutes before serving.

Variation: *Try using arugula instead of asparagus, and cooked pancetta instead of prosciutto.*

Prep time: *15 minutes*
Hands-off cooking time: *10 minutes*
Serves 4

Per ¼ pizza: 485 calories, 19 g fat, 7 g saturated fat, 24 g protein, 56 g carbs, 3 g fiber, 1 g sugar, 813 mg sodium

 *Omit prosciutto*

Seafood Paella

Paella is the famous Spanish dish originating from the Valencia region, featuring seafood simmering in saffron rice. This easy one-pan recipe is flavorful and festive. Pair paella with a fruity pitcher of sangria (page 204) and a few friends.

1 cup Arborio rice, or any short or medium grain rice

2 Tbsp extra virgin olive oil, divided

2 refrigerated Garlic & Herb Chicken Sausages, sliced

2 ½ cups water

½ cup Chunky Salsa, or your favorite salsa

1 tsp Spanish Saffron (half the jar)

1 pound frozen small scallops, thawed

1 pound frozen uncooked medium or large shrimp, thawed (tail on or off)

1 cup frozen shelled edamame or peas

½ cup dry white wine

1   Heat 1 Tbsp oil on high heat in a wide deep saucepan or skillet.

2   Sauté sausage for until browned and transfer to a plate.

3   Pat scallops dry. In the same pan, sauté scallops until opaque, about 1-2 minutes, and transfer to a plate.

4   Add remaining oil to pan. Add rice and stir to coat with oil. Stir in water, salsa, and saffron to pan. Bring to a simmer and cover, reducing heat to low. After 15 minutes, when most of the water is absorbed, add shrimp, edamame, and wine, stirring slightly to combine.

5   Increase heat and simmer uncovered for an additional 5 minutes, until shrimp becomes opaque and cooked and rice has absorbed nearly all the liquid. Gently stir in scallops and sausage. Serve immediately.

Prep and cooking time: *20-25 minutes*
Serves 6

Note: *Paella is traditionally made with short grain rice. Arborio is the closest to authentic paella rice such as bomba. If you prefer a light and fluffy paella, substitute long grain rice such as basmati.*

Per serving: 383 calories, 11 g fat, 2 g saturated fat, 38 g protein, 30 g carbs, 2 g fiber, 2 g sugar, 527 mg sodium

Curried Chicken Pitas

This is no ordinary chicken salad sandwich. Grapes add a burst of juicy flavor, and cashews give a nice crunch to the creamy curry and chutney dressing. The filling can be stuffed in pita pockets, rolled in tortillas, or placed in a baguette.

3 cups cooked chicken, such as refrigerated charbroiled Just Chicken, cut into bite-size pieces

½ cup Thai Yellow Curry Sauce

¼ cup Mango Ginger Chutney

1 cup grapes, halved

½ cup whole cashews

1 scallion, chopped

8 lettuce leaves, such as Just the Leaves of Green Leaf Lettuce

4 white or whole wheat pitas

1   Mix curry and chutney until well blended. Add chicken and toss to coat. Stir in grapes, cashews, and scallion.

2   Cut pitas in half. Stuff each half with chicken salad mixture and a lettuce leaf.

Variation: Try substituting chopped apples for the grapes and pecans for the cashews.

Prep time: *15 minutes*
Serves 4

Per serving: 493 calories, 15 g fat, 4 g saturated fat, 39 g protein, 49 g carbs, 6 g fiber, 17 g sugar, 734 mg sodium

Cooking with All Things Trader Joe's

Wine Suggestion:

Kono Marlborough Sauvignon Blanc, a clean refreshing wine from New Zealand full of citrus and apple flavor, goes well with this mild curry.

Beer Suggestion:

Serve with Trader Joe's
Bohemian Style Lager,
a sweet and aromatic beer.
If you're in the mood for wine,
try **Geyser Peak Sauvignon
Blanc,** light and crisp for easy
drinking.

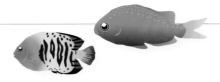

California Fish Taco

A fish taco? Welcome to a favorite of the California beach crowd. If you've never tried one, you'll soon wonder why not. We've created a fast and fresh-tasting version of this legendary treat. Serve with chips, salsa, and a cold *cerveza*!

6 medium flour tortillas

1 box (about 6 fillets) frozen Oven Ready Breaded Cod Fillets or other breaded fillets

3 cups Stir Fry Vegetables (Napa cabbage version) or shredded white cabbage

1 ½ Tbsp refrigerated Cilantro Dressing

Juice from one lime

1 cup chopped tomato

Fresh cilantro for garnish

1 Cook fish fillets according to package instructions. Place one fillet on each open tortilla.

2 Toss vegetables with dressing and divide among tortillas, about ½ cup per tortilla.

3 Add a squeeze of lime and some tomatoes to each tortilla, garnish with cilantro, and serve immediately.

Prep time: *10 minutes*
Hands-off cooking time: *20 minutes (for the fish)*
Makes 6 tacos

Per taco: 333 calories, 10 g fat, 1 g saturated fat, 14 g protein, 43 g carbs, 3 g fiber, 3 g sugar, 452 mg sodium

Korean Bool Kogi on Rice Sticks

Bool Kogi means "fire meat" in Korean – seasoned meat grilled over a hot fire. A little sweet and somewhat garlicky, Bool Kogi is tender, juicy, and full of flavor. We've paired this all-time Korean favorite with seasoned rice noodles for a one-dish meal.

1 (1.5-2 lb) pkg Korean Bool Kogi meat, available refrigerated ready-to-cook, or frozen Korean Style Beef Short Ribs

6 oz Rice Sticks noodles (about half the package) or other Asian rice noodles

3 Tbsp soy sauce

1 Tbsp toasted sesame oil

1 Tbsp sugar

2 cloves garlic, crushed, or 2 cubes frozen Crushed Garlic

1 carrot, shredded, or 1 cup bagged Shredded Carrots

1 cup sliced mushrooms, cooked or raw

2 green onions, thinly sliced

1   Prepare meat according to package instructions. Once meat is cooked, remove from heat and cover with foil for 10 minutes. Allowing the meat to rest under foil keeps it juicy.

2   Cook noodles according to package instructions and drain.

3   Whisk soy sauce, sesame oil, sugar, and garlic until combined. Pour dressing onto cooked noodles and toss well to coat. Stir in carrots and mushrooms.

4   Slice meat diagonally into thick strips.

5   To serve, arrange noodles on platter. Place sliced meat on top of noodles. Garnish with green onions.

Prep and cooking time: *20 minutes*
Serves 4

Per serving: 544 calories, 24 g fat, 9 g saturated fat, 27 g protein, 6 g carbs, 2 g fiber, 10 g sugar, 1265 mg sodium

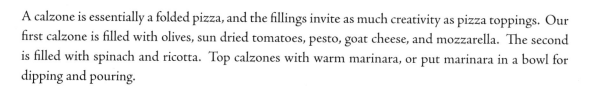

Calzone with Olives and Sun Dried Tomatoes

A calzone is essentially a folded pizza, and the fillings invite as much creativity as pizza toppings. Our first calzone is filled with olives, sun dried tomatoes, pesto, goat cheese, and mozzarella. The second is filled with spinach and ricotta. Top calzones with warm marinara, or put marinara in a bowl for dipping and pouring.

---

1 (1-lb) bag refrigerated Ready to Bake Pizza Dough

2 Tbsp refrigerated Genova Pesto

2 Tbsp Julienne Sliced Sun Dried Tomatoes

4 Tbsp Crumbled Goat Cheese

10 pitted Kalamata olives, sliced in half

⅔ cup Shredded Mozzarella Cheese

½ cup Tomato & Basil Marinara or your favorite marinara sauce, heated

Shredded fresh basil for garnish

1   Preheat oven to 450° F, preferably with a pizza stone inside.

2   Separate dough into two balls. Flour surface and use your hands to flatten and stretch each ball of dough to an 8-inch circle.

3   Spread pesto on half of each circle, avoiding the edges. Add tomatoes, olives, goat cheese, and mozzarella.

4   Fold in half, forming the classic half-moon shape. Gently but firmly pinch edges together, crimping with your fingers or a fork.

5   Bake calzones on pizza stone or oiled baking sheet for 20 minutes until tops are golden.

Prep time: *10 minutes*
Hands-off cooking time: *20 minutes*
**Makes 2 large calzones*

Per half-calzone serving: 466 calories, 17 g fat, 5 g saturated fat, 18 g protein, 60 g carbs, 3 g fiber, 3 g sugar, 699 mg sodium

Cooking with All Things Trader Joe's

Spinach Ricotta Calzone

1 (1-lb) bag refrigerated Ready to Bake Pizza Dough

2 cups frozen chopped spinach, measured while frozen

⅓ cup refrigerated Grilled Artichoke & Parmesan Dip

1 cup ricotta cheese

1   Prepare dough as before.

2   Rinse spinach under cool water until thawed. Drain, squeezing out water with your hands.

3   Place spinach in a small bowl and stir in artichoke dip. Place half the spinach mixture on one side of dough, top with half the ricotta, then fold over and crimp. Repeat for second calzone and bake as before.

Per half-calzone serving: 382 calories, 5 g fat, 2 g saturated fat, 19 g protein, 60 g carbs, 3 g fiber, 5 g sugar, 530 mg sodium

Wine Suggestion:

Enjoy your calzones with a soft, smooth, and fruity California Pinot Noir, such as Red Truck California Pinot Noir.

Chipotle Turkey Chili

On a cold night, warm your body and soul with a big bowl of homemade chili. Refried beans thicken the chili, giving it long-cooked texture and flavor in just minutes. Chipotle salsa adds a kick of heat, while a splash of barbecue sauce balances the spice with a touch of smoky sweetness.

1 ¼ lb ground turkey (one package)

1 medium onion, chopped, or 1 ½ cups bagged Freshly Diced Onions

1 Tbsp olive oil

1 tsp ground cumin

1 (28-oz) can diced tomatoes

1 (15-oz) can black beans or kidney beans

1 can refried black beans or pinto beans (for a thinner chili, use half the can)

½ cup Chipotle Salsa

¼ cup barbecue sauce

Sour cream (optional)

Fancy Shredded Mexican Blend cheese (optional)

1   Heat olive oil in medium saucepan over medium heat. Cook onions 5 minutes. Add ground turkey and cook until brown, breaking it up as it cooks. Add ground cumin and cook 1 minute longer.

2   Add remaining ingredients. Refried beans need to be broken up and stirred into the chili until dissolved.

3   When chili comes to a boil, lower heat and simmer for 10 minutes.

4   Garnish with sour cream and cheese.

Prep time: *10 minutes*
Hands-off cooking time: *15 minutes*
Serves 4

Per serving: 387 calories, 4 g fat, 0 g saturated fat, 44 g protein, 40 g carbs, 7 g fiber, 11 g sugar, 913 mg sodium

Gluten Free

Penne Pepperonata with Shrimp and Asparagus

Minutes to the table! The frozen prepared pasta in this recipe makes a solid foundation for building a more complex and jazzed up entrée. Shrimp and green veggies combined with the pasta in a creamy tomato-based sauce make a substantial and satisfying meal. This dish is one of those healthy quickies that can be made and served in minutes. It's not nearly as spicy as the name implies and makes for a very kid-friendly meal.

---

1 (16-oz) bag frozen Penne Pepperonata

1 ½ cup frozen or fresh asparagus, cut into 2-inch pieces

½ cup frozen peas

1 ½ cup frozen Large or Medium Cooked Tail-Off Shrimp

1   Don't bother thawing any ingredients.

2   Toss all ingredients in a wide saucepan and sauté on medium high heat until completely heated through.

Prep and cooking time: *10 minutes*
Serves 4

Per serving: 308 calories, 6 g fat, 2 g saturated fat, 21 g protein, 44 g carbs, 5 g fiber, 5 g sugar, 302 mg sodium

Blue Corn Taco Salad Olé!

There is no such thing as a taco salad in Mexico, but this Mexican-inspired salad using the contents of a taco is a favorite on this side of the border. This hearty salad has plenty of crunch from warm tortilla chips and a familiar but distinctive flavor from homemade salsa vinaigrette. No need to measure to measure any of the suggested ingredients precisely – improvise and throw in any salad items you have on hand.

---

3 cups cooked meat (Pollo Asado Autentico, cooked and shredded, or 1 lb ground turkey cooked with Taco Seasoning)

½ cup canned black beans

1 (7-oz) bag Baked Blue Corn Tortilla Chips

1 (9-oz) bag Very American Salad (a blend of iceberg, romaine, and red cabbage)

½ cup frozen Roasted Corn, thawed, or canned corn

1 cup fresh diced tomatoes or cherry tomatoes

½ cup chopped fresh avocado or refrigerated Avocado's Number Guacamole

¼ cup chopped onions or green onions

1 cup Fancy Shredded Mexican Blend cheese

½ cup sour cream

½ cup refrigerated Cilantro Dressing or Homemade Salsa Vinaigrette (recipe follows)

1 Preheat oven to 300° F.

2 Place tortilla chips in oven for 5 minutes to make them warm and crispy. Heat meat and black beans, either in microwave or pan.

3 Place salad in the bottom of a large salad bowl. Add corn, tomatoes, avocados, and onions.

4 Top with warm chips, meat, and black beans. Sprinkle evenly with shredded cheese. Place a big dollop of sour cream on top.

5 Pour dressing on top and toss. Serve immediately.

Prep and cooking time: 10 minutes
Serves 4

Homemade Salsa Vinaigrette

1 cup refrigerated Mild Salsa, or your favorite fresh or bottled salsa

½ cup olive oil

¼ cup fresh lemon juice

½ tsp ground cumin

½ tsp salt

2 Tbsp chopped cilantro

 Use seasoned ground turkey or chicken. Pollo Asado Autentico contains a gluten ingredient

 Omit meat or use meatless substitute

1   Whisk all ingredients until combined.

Per serving: 492 calories, 17 g fat, 4 g saturated fat, 28 g protein, 61 g carbs, 9 g fiber, 8 g sugar, 669 mg sodium

Corny-Copia Bean and Veggie Casserole

This dish is a complex and substantial vegetarian entrée, with layered beans, roasted veggies, briny olives, and a cornbread topping. It was adapted from a recipe in the *Moosewood Cookbook*, which had a prep time of 1 ½ hours. We've come up with a version we like just as well, with a fraction of the prep time.

1 medium yellow onion, chopped, or 1 ½ cups bagged Freshly Diced Onions

1 clove garlic, crushed, or 1 cube frozen Crushed Garlic

2 Tbsp extra virgin olive oil

1 tsp ground cumin

1 (15-oz) can pinto beans, drained completely

½ cup plain yogurt

1 (12-oz) jar Fire Roasted Red & Yellow Peppers, drained and chopped

1 (10-oz) jar Green Olive Tapenade or other olive tapenade/bruschetta

1 (15-oz) box Cornbread Mix, prepared to instructions and set aside

1   Preheat oven to 375° F.

2   Sauté onions, garlic and cumin in olive oil until onions are soft and translucent. Set pan aside to cool.

3   Bottom layer: Mix beans and yogurt in a large bowl. Add cooked onions, stirring to mix. Place in 8 x 8-inch baking dish. Flatten with spatula.

4   Middle layer: Mix together peppers and tapenade; spread over bean mixture.

5   Top casserole with a thin layer of cornbread batter (about ⅔ of the mix —use the rest to make muffins for breakfast the next day). Spoon cornbread batter evenly and thinly over the top, taking care not to disturb the layers.

6   Bake uncovered for 35-40 minutes or until cornbread is fully cooked and golden brown.

Variation: *For the middle layer, substitute 2 cups of Oven Roasted Vegetables (see p. 186)*

Prep time: *15 minutes*
Hands-off cooking time: *35-40 minutes*
Serves 9

Per serving: 437 calories, 21 g fat, 1 g saturated fat, 7 g protein, 54 g carbs, 4 g fiber, 20 g sugar, 829 mg sodium

Vegetarian

Saag Paneer Lasagna

This dish is fusion cooking at its most eclectic. Most people might not pair Indian and Italian cooking, but the combination of spinach and ricotta is the crossover reminiscent of Saag Paneer and spinach lasagna. This tasty twist on two classics is delicious without being heavy.

---

1 pkg dry "no boil" lasagna noodles

2 (15-oz) jars Masala Simmer Sauce

1 (16-oz) bag frozen chopped spinach

1 cup frozen peas, thawed

1 (15-oz) container ricotta cheese

1 (16-oz) bag Shredded Mozzarella Cheese

1   Preheat oven to 375° F.

2   Spray or wipe a 9 x 13–inch baking pan with olive oil. Spread a few Tbsp Masala sauce on the bottom. Add a single layer of lasagna noodles.

3   Thaw spinach, or place it in a colander under cool water until thawed. Drain well, squeezing out excess water with your hands.

4   In a bowl, combine spinach, peas, and remaining Masala sauce. Mix well.

5   Layer ¼ of spinach mixture over noodles, followed by ⅓ of the ricotta and another layer of noodles. Press down lightly to compact layers. Repeat layering 2 more times. Spread final ¼ of spinach mixture on noodles and top with mozzarella.

6   Cover loosely with foil and bake for 25 minutes. Remove foil and cook 20 minutes longer, allowing cheese to get bubbly and golden.

Prep time: *10 minutes*
Hands-off cooking time: *45 minutes*
Serves 8

Per serving: 498 calories, 19 g fat, 9 g saturated fat, 33 g protein, 55 g carbs, 5 g fiber, 14 g sugar, 908 mg sodium

Wine Suggestion:

Choose a spicy Zinfandel, such as **Cline Zinfandel**, to match the briny richness of this dish. This wine has dark berry and spice notes with a long vanilla oak finish.

Caper-lovers Chicken and Eggplant

We love easy dishes that you can quickly assemble and toss in the oven. If you love the salty, piquant taste of capers, this is a dish you have to try. Serve with a salad or a side of pasta.

---

2 boneless, skinless chicken breasts

1 Tbsp olive oil

1 medium-sized eggplant, peeled and cubed

1 (14-oz) container refrigerated Fresh Bruschetta Sauce

2 Tbsp capers

¼ cup chopped green olives

1 Preheat oven to 350° F.

2 Spread oil in bottom of 8 x 10-inch baking dish. Add eggplant to dish.

3 Bruschetta sauce will have a layer of oil on top. Drizzle chicken with this oil, coating well, and place chicken on eggplant layer.

4 Stir capers and olives into bruschetta, and spoon mixture on top of chicken and eggplant.

5 Bake uncovered for 40 minutes or until chicken is done. Very large breasts may require an extra 5-10 minutes.

Prep time: *10 minutes*
Hands-off cooking time: *40 minutes*
Serves 4

Per serving: 243 calories, 12 g fat, 1 g saturated fat, 26 g protein, 10 g carbs, 4 g fiber, 6 g sugar, 327 mg sodium

Gluten Free

Spicy Szechuan Tofu

This dish was inspired by Ma Po Tofu, a spicy specialty from the Szechuan province of China. Although Ma Po Tofu is usually made with ground pork, we think this version is just as tasty with turkey or beef. Don't say you don't like tofu until you've tried this dish – you may become a convert!

1 (16-oz or 19-oz) pkg firm tofu, cut into ½-inch cubes

½ lb ground turkey or beef

1 clove garlic, crushed, or 1 cube frozen Crushed Garlic

1 tsp crushed ginger

1 cup frozen peas

½ cup General Tsao Stir Fry Sauce

1 Tbsp soy sauce

1 tsp toasted sesame oil

2 green onions, chopped

1   Cook turkey in a skillet or wok, breaking it up as it cooks. Add garlic, ginger, and peas; cook 2 minutes longer.

2   Add tofu, stir fry sauce, soy sauce, and sesame oil. Cook for 3 minutes or until heated through.

3   Add green onions and remove from heat. Serve over steamed white rice.

Prep and cooking time: *15 minutes*
Serves 4

Per serving: 303 calories, 13 g fat, 2 g saturated fat, 26 g protein, 23 g carbs, 3 g fiber, 17 g sugar, 560 mg sodium

 Use meatless product

Wine Suggestion:

Spicy Asian dishes pair well with a medium-dry Riesling or Gewürztraminer. Try J.W. Morris Gewürztraminer, a sweet, peachy, and aromatic wine that pairs well with this spicy dish.

Vegetable Tikka Masala

Tikka Masala is one of our favorite Indian dishes. Masala is a slightly spicy tomato-based sauce that is commonly believed to be a product of Indian-British fusion cooking, although the origins are somewhat unclear. When you add yogurt to it, you get a Tikka Masala sauce that is nicely balanced with the cooling taste of yogurt, complex and very creamy, but not at all heavy. It is great over plain steamed basmati rice or quinoa, along with some Tandoori Naan (available fresh or frozen in several flavors).

---

1 (15-oz) jar Masala Simmer Sauce

1 (12-oz) bag Cauliflower Florets or 3 cups cauliflower, cut into bite-size pieces

1 medium zucchini, unpeeled, diced into ½ inch chunks (about 1 cup)

½ cup frozen peas

¾ cup canned garbanzo beans

½ cup carrots, thinly sliced (optional)

½ cup plain yogurt, such as Plain Cream Line Yogurt

1 Pour masala sauce in a wide large saucepan over medium heat.

2 Add cauliflower, zucchini, peas, garbanzo beans, and carrots. Stir until all ingredients are coated.

3 Once simmering, cover pan and turn heat to medium-low. Simmer for an additional 12-15 minutes or until cauliflower and carrots are just tender.

4 Ladle out ½ cup or more of the curry and mix into the yogurt (this will temper the yogurt, so that it doesn't curdle in the hot curry). Stir yogurt mixture into the pan, bring to a simmer again, and then remove from heat.

Prep time: 5 minutes
Hands off cooking time: 15-20 minutes
Serves 4

Per serving: 175 calories, 5 g fat, 1 g saturated fat, 9 g protein, 27 g carbs, 7 g fiber, 14 g sugar, 592 mg sodium

Take a Stab at Cheese Fondue

Fondue is a great way to entertain. It's the indoors equivalent of a campfire – good friends gathered around a warm pot. Although the display is impressive, it is simple to make and can all be prepped ahead of time. Cheese fondue is usually served with cubed bread, but we like to include colorful veggie dippers as well. Vegetables ready to microwave in their own bags reduce prep work to just minutes. Choose any dippers you like, as long as they are firm enough to be stabbed with a fondue fork.

Cheese Sauce

½ lb Emmentaler cheese, grated

½ lb Gruyère cheese, grated
(Cave-Aged is especially flavorful)

¼ lb Havarti cheese, grated (optional)

1 Tbsp flour

1 clove of garlic, halved

1 ½ cups dry white wine

Fondue Dippers

Crusty bread, cut into 1-inch cubes

Broccoli florets, cauliflower florets

Baby carrots, baby squash, baby zucchini

Fingerling potatoes

Sugar snap peas, green beans

Cherry tomatoes

Ham, cut into chunky cubes

1 To prepare vegetables (any selection of broccoli, cauliflower, squash, zucchini, potatoes, sugar snap peas), simply microwave in packaged bags, or boil in salted water until crisp-tender. Arrange dippers on a platter and set aside until ready to serve.

2 Mix cheeses in a bowl. Toss with flour. This is all you should do before guests arrive. Cheese fondue should be prepared just before serving.

3 When guests are ready, rub the inside of a fondue pot or saucepan with cut sides of garlic. Discard remaining garlic. Add wine and bring to a simmer. Reduce heat to low and fold in cheese, stirring constantly until all cheese melts. Do not let boil or cheese will harden.

4 Arm guests with fondue forks and serve fondue with a big platter of dippers.

Note: *If you have Kirsch (a clear cherry liqueur), add 2 tsp at the very end.*

Prep time: *10-20 minutes*
Serves 6 good friends

 Omit bread

Per serving of cheese sauce: 439 calories, 31 g fat, 21 g saturated fat, 24 g protein, 3 g carbs, 0 g fiber, 0 g sugar, 194 mg sodium

 Omit ham

Wine Suggestion:

Go for something that is bright and acidic, but with enough fruity and earthy flavors to go with cave-aged cheeses like Gruyère. We like Geyser Peak Winery Sauvignon Blanc. Or try Gloria Ferrer Sonoma Brut Sparkling Wine if you like the bubbles!

Chickety Chinese Chicken Salad

We dare you to try eating this dish without having the famed Barenaked Ladies tune running through your head: "Chickety China the Chinese Chicken…" This dish is as delish as it is fun, with vibrant colors and yummy peanut butter dressing. Kids and kid-like adults may not realize you're sneaking healthy vegetables into their meals. Serve this salad cold on a warm summer day.

---

3 cups cooked chicken, such as refrigerated charbroiled Just Chicken, cut into bite-size pieces

⅓ cup Soyaki or Veri Veri Teriyaki

⅓ cup creamy salted peanut butter

1 Tbsp toasted sesame oil

⅓ cup water

½ of a red bell pepper, sliced into strips

½ of a yellow bell pepper, sliced into strips

1 cup snow peas

2 green onions, chopped

½ cup cashews

1 Whisk Soyaki, peanut butter, and sesame oil until blended. Add water and mix well.

2 Place chicken, vegetables, and cashews in a large bowl. Add peanut sauce and stir to coat evenly.

Prep time: *15 minutes*
Serves 4

Per serving: 492 calories, 26 g fat, 4 g saturated fat, 40 g protein, 22 g carbs, 5 g fiber, 10 g sugar, 820 mg sodium

 Use GF teriyaki sauce, such as San-J or Seal Sama Teriyaki sauce, available at other grocers

Baja Quesadillas

Don't be afraid to experiment with quesadillas. A little "queso" inside a tortilla and you've got the base for mealtime creativity. Try beans, veggies, olives, chicken, marinated/baked tofu, and choose from all kinds of toppings like greens, avocado, sour cream and salsas. You really can put almost anything inside a quesadilla (see our Perfectly Peared Gorgonzola Quesadilla on page 23 if you don't believe us!). A cast iron pan is really nice for retaining heat and cooking a quesadilla, but almost any pan will do.

1 medium flour tortilla

½ cup cooked chicken, such as refrigerated charbroiled Just Chicken, chopped

2 Tbsp Chunky Salsa

½ cup Fancy Shredded Mexican Blend cheese

2 Tbsp Avocado's Number Guacamole

⅓ cup chopped cherry tomatoes or chopped tomato

1 Tbsp chopped fresh cilantro

1   Place tortilla on lightly oiled skillet over medium-low heat.

2   Place chicken on one half of tortilla and cover with salsa. Sprinkle cheese liberally over entire tortilla.

3   Heat until cheese melts. Dollop guacamole inside, sprinkle in cherry tomatoes and cilantro, and fold over. Flip once with spatula to heat through.

4   Cut in half and serve.

Tip: Don't own a pan? Don't own a stovetop? No problem! Quesadillas can also be easily prepared in the oven. Turn on your oven broiler to low or preheat oven to 350° F. Lay flour tortilla on a baking sheet and prepare in the same way, placing in the oven open-faced for about 5 minutes or until cheese is melted. Fold and serve.

Prep and cooking time: *10-15 minutes*
Serves 1

Per serving: 561 calories, 30 g fat, 14 g saturated fat,
36 g protein, 29 g carbs, 3 g fiber, 1 g sugar, 915 mg sodium

 Use brown rice tortilla

 Use Chicken-less Strips

Spinach & Artichoke Chicken Crepes

It's no wonder the French love crepes! Light, chewy, and delicately lacy, crepes are versatile and oh-so-chic. They are great around-the-clock: filled with breakfast items, lunch or dinner fare, or even fruit for dessert. This version uses fully prepared items to make assembly a snap, but the beauty is you can fill crepes with any leftovers you have on hand.

10 ready-made crepes

1 ½ cups cooked chicken, such as refrigerated charbroiled Just Chicken, sliced

1 (8-oz) box frozen Creamy Spinach & Artichoke Dip, cooked according to package instructions

1   Warm crepes according to package instructions. To assemble crepes, spread a heaping spoonful of spinach and artichoke dip on one half of the crepe. Top with several slices of chicken. Roll crepe and place on baking tray or cookie sheet.

2   Place assembled crepes in a 200° F oven to keep warm.

Prep and cooking time: *5 minutes*
Makes 10 crepes

Per crepe: 162 calories, 4 g fat, 2 g saturated fat, 11 g protein,
19 g carbs, 1 g fiber, 2 g sugar, 271 mg sodium

South of the Border Pizza

A cool layer of guacamole on top of yummy hot beans, melted cheese, salsa, and a thin crust. A unique cold/hot pizza that makes so much sense. Don't skip the cilantro—it really completes this pizza!

1 (1-lb) bag refrigerated Almost Whole Wheat Pizza Dough

1 (15-oz) can pinto beans, drained completely

½ cup Chunky Salsa

1 cup Shredded 3 Cheese Blend

1 cup (one tray) refrigerated Avocado's Number Guacamole

¼ cup chopped fresh cilantro

1. Preheat oven to 500° F or as high as your oven goes, preferably with a pizza stone inside.

2. Roll dough into a 12-inch circle on a lightly floured surface. Cover dough with salsa, beans, and cheese, in that order.

3. Transfer to pizza stone or baking sheet. Bake for 10 minutes or until cheese is bubbly.

4. Remove pizza from the oven and slice. Spread guacamole over each slice while hot, and sprinkle cilantro on top. Serve immediately.

Note: *Spread guacamole only over the slices you're planning on eating, since guacamole will oxidize and turn brown on leftovers.*

Prep time: *10 minutes*
Hands-off cooking time: *10 minutes*
Serves 4

Per ¼-pizza: 562 calories, 19 g fat, 6 g saturated fat, 22 g protein, 72 g carbs, 16 g fiber, 2 g sugar, 1076 mg sodium

Wine Suggestion:

You can't go wrong with a well-rounded and jammy wine like **Estancia Pinot Noir** that will balance the rich creaminess of this dish.

Okey-Gnocchi with Pancetta & Peas

Gnocchi, Italian for "lumps" or "knots," are tender bite-size lumps of potato-based dough. Their distinctive shape, with ridges on one side like a seashell, gives the sauce a surface to cling onto. Trader Joe's frozen gnocchi, with creamy Gorgonzola cheese sauce pieces right in the ready-to-cook package, is scrumptious on its own. Adding pancetta and peas makes it even better.

1 (16-oz) bag frozen Gnocchi Alla Gorgonzola

2 oz Pancetta mini-cubes, about half the package, or ½ cup chopped ham

½ cup frozen peas or 1 cup frozen chopped spinach

1 Tbsp chopped fresh basil or 1 cube frozen Chopped Basil (optional)

1   Cook pancetta over medium-high heat until browned. Place on a paper towel to drain grease.

2   Pour entire package of gnocchi in a medium saucepan and cook for 5 minutes until cheese is almost melted. Add pancetta and frozen peas; continue cooking for 3 minutes longer.

3   Stir in basil.

Prep and cooking time: 10 minutes
Serves 4

Per serving: 318 calories, 15 g fat, 3 g saturated fat, 6 g protein, 35 g carbs, 4 g fiber, 11 g sugar, 963 mg sodium

 Omit pancetta

Grilled Yogurt Dill Chicken Skewers

Looking for juicy chicken and flavorful veggies? Marinate and grill them! You can use your oven or grill to make these delicious and tender chicken kabobs. For a really easy and quick meal, assemble skewers ahead of time and cover with plastic wrap. When you're ready, start some rice or pasta and toss skewers in the oven or on the grill.

2-3 skinless, boneless chicken breasts (about 1 lb), cut into 1-inch chunks

1 cup yogurt

2 tsp dried dill

½ a medium onion, thinly sliced

½ tsp salt

¼ tsp black pepper

2 zucchini, unpeeled and cut crosswise into ½-inch pieces

1 (10-oz) container whole white mushrooms

1 large (or two small) red bell pepper, seeds and pith removed, cut into 1-inch pieces

10-12 cherry tomatoes

1   Combine yogurt, dill, onion, salt, and pepper.

2   Marinate chicken chunks in yogurt mixture for a few hours or overnight in the fridge.

3   Using long wooden or metal skewers, assemble skewers one by one, alternating ingredients. Dispose of the marinade you used for the chicken.

4   Cook on the grill or use an oven.

Oven Instructions

1   Preheat oven to 400° F.

2   Place skewers across a foil-lined 9 x 13-inch oven-safe pan.

3   Cook in the center of the oven for 15-20 minutes or until chicken juices run clear when cut.

Prep time: *15 minutes*
Hands off cooking time: *20 minutes*
Makes ten 10-inch skewers

Per skewer: 64 calories, 2 g fat, 1 g saturated fat, 11 g protein, 3 g carbs, 1 g fiber, 1 g sugar, 90 mg sodium

Sweet and Tart Cherry Rice

This middle eastern rice dish is flavored with saffron, onion, and cherries. Like many "sweet and sour" flavors from the Middle East, sour cherries are perfect for creating that balance in this dish. The method for making this dish requires boiling to soften the rice, then steaming with all ingredients combined. Cooking the rice twice prevents it from forming an indistinct mush. The end result is a beautiful and delicious jeweled rice, with color variations accented by saffron and cherries.

2 ½ cups uncooked basmati rice

1 tsp Spanish Saffron (half the jar)

1 (24.7-oz) jar Dark Morello Cherries, drain off ½ cup liquid and discard

½ cup Dried Pitted Tart Montmorency Cherries or dried cranberries

3 Tbsp unsalted butter, divided

2 Tbsp extra virgin olive oil, divided

1 large yellow onion, chopped, or 2 cups bagged Freshly Diced Onions

1 ½ tsp salt, divided

2 cups (½ lb) cooked chicken, such as refrigerated charbroiled Just Chicken, shredded

1 Place saffron threads in a small cup with 1 Tbsp of hot water and stir.

2 Rinse rice in water and drain. Place rice in a large pot and add 8 cups of water and 1 tsp salt. Once the water is boiling, boil for about 4 minutes. Drain rice.

3 While rice cooks, combine dried and jarred cherries with liquid in saucepan over medium-low heat.

4 In a skillet, sauté onion in 1 Tbsp butter and 1 Tbsp olive oil until soft, about 5 minutes. Add ½ tsp salt.

5 Now you have the 3 components to start layering: rice, cherry mixture, and onion. Place 1 Tbsp butter and 1 Tbsp olive oil in large pot used for rice. Build 3 layers of each by alternating rice, cherry mixture, and onion in pot, forming a mound.

6 Pour saffron water and any remaining cherry juice over rice layers and dot with remaining butter. Don't stir or disturb the pot. Cover with a lid and steam for 35 minutes on low heat until rice is done. Add chicken and steam for an additional 5 minutes

7 Scoop out onto a platter, gently combining ingredients.

Prep time: *20 minutes*
Hands-off cooking time: *40*
Serves 8

G Gluten Free   Vegetarian   *Omit chicken or use Chicken-less trips*

Per serving: 443 calories, 10 g fat, 4 g saturated fat, 15 g protein, 60 g carbs, 1 g fiber, 14 g sugar, 270 mg sodium

Red Curry Halibut

Halibut is a mild fish with a great texture, perfect for showing off a flavorful curry sauce. Serve with jasmine rice and Wilted Spinach (page 179). Or, if you want to make this a one-dish meal, add vegetables such as snow peas, zucchini, carrots, or whatever you have on hand. Place vegetables in the pan with fish and cook together.

4 halibut or snapper filets (if using frozen, thaw in fridge or under running cold water)

1 cup Thai Red Curry Sauce

1 Tbsp fresh lime juice

2 Tbsp chopped fresh basil

2 Tbsp chopped fresh cilantro

1   Place curry sauce in a saucepan large enough to fit all fillets. Heat sauce over medium heat until it starts to boil.

2   Add fish, spooning sauce over fillets to cover and season all over. Cover and cook 6-7 minutes or until fish flakes easily when tested with a fork. Do not overcook.

3   Stir lime juice, basil, and cilantro into sauce. To serve, plate fish and pour sauce on top.

Prep time: 5 minutes
Hands-off cooking time: 10 minutes
Serves 4

Per serving: 218 calories, 9 g fat, 4 g saturated fat, 24 g protein, 8 g carbs, 1 g fiber, 3 g sugar, 981 mg sodium

Anytime Mediterranean Pasta

This pasta dish can be your fallback option any time, even if your fridge is nearly bare. Just keep a bag of pasta, a bag of pine nuts, and a few jarred sauces on hand in your pantry. Parmesan cheese will keep for a long time in your fridge.

3 cups dry fusilli or penne pasta (we used Penne Rigata, about ½ a bag)

½ cup pitted Kalamata olives

2 Tbsp Julienne Sliced Sun Dried Tomatoes

⅓ cup toasted pine nuts

2 Tbsp Pesto alla Genovese Basil Pesto

¼ cup grated or shredded Parmesan cheese

1   Cook pasta according to package instructions and drain.

2   Stir in remaining ingredients, topping with Parmesan as desired.

Prep and cooking time: 15 minutes
Serves 4

Per serving: 369 calories, 17 g fat, 2 g saturated fat, 8 g protein, 48 g carbs, 3 g fiber, 1 g sugar, 314 mg sodium

Use brown rice pasta

Wine Suggestion:

With the olives and tomatoes in this dish, try a full fruity wine with oak flavors, such as **Baron Herzog Merlot**.

Mole Chicken Enchiladas with Pecans

Traditional mole (pronounced MOH-lay) is an intricate smooth sauce typically served with poultry. Mole usually takes all day to prepare, and every Mexican family has their own secret recipe. Trader Joe's mole tastes like homemade, and with a few untraditional ingredients, we've discovered a great version of chicken mole enchiladas. A filling made of cream cheese, pecans, and red pepper really complements and harmonizes with the smoky, spicy, sweet taste of mole. Vegetarian? Just leave out the chicken or substitute it with Oven Roasted Vegetables (page 186).

4 cups (1 lb) cooked chicken, or a 1-lb container refrigerated charbroiled Just Chicken, shredded

⅔ container (⅔ cup) whipped cream cheese

½ cup pecans, chopped

1 (12-oz) jar Fire Roasted Red Peppers, sliced in 1-inch strips

1 (12-oz) jar Red Mole

6 medium flour tortillas

Sour cream or plain yogurt (optional)

1   Preheat oven to 350° F.

2   Place chicken and cream cheese in a bowl and stir together. Add pecans and stir.

3   To assemble, place 1 super-heaping Tbsp of mixture toward one end of tortilla, and spread over ¾ of tortilla. Place a couple of red pepper strips down the center. Starting from the filled end, roll tightly and place seam side down on oiled baking dish.

4   Once all tortillas are finished, top with mole, cover pan with foil or a lid, and bake for 20 minutes.

5   Top with a few whole pecans and sour cream or yogurt.

Prep time: *15 minutes*
Hands-off cooking time: *20 minutes*
Serves 6

Per serving: 525 calories, 27 g fat, 7 g saturated fat, 33 g protein, 38 g carbs, 4 g fiber, 10 g sugar, 943 mg sodium

Easy Tofu Stir Fry

It's good to have a wide variety of easy recipes using fresh vegetables that can be a quick 10-minutes-to-the-table dinner, like this easy tofu-based stir fry. Tofu is lightly flavored with sesame oil and gets a tiny bit of heat from chili oil. Vegetables are crisp and vibrant in the tasty soy-teriyaki sauce. Serve over brown or white rice.

½ brick tofu (regular), cut into ½-inch cubes and drained

1 Tbsp olive oil

1 tsp toasted sesame oil

10 drops chili oil

4 cups Stir Fry Vegetables (Napa cabbage variety) or substitute an equivalent amount of broccoli florets, white cabbage, and/or bok choy

⅓ cup Soyaki or Veri Veri Teriyaki

1   Heat a wok or wide saucepan on high and add all oils. Add tofu and stir-fry for 2 minutes.

2   Reduce heat to medium-high, add vegetables and Soyaki, and continue to stir-fry for an additional 3 minutes or until broccoli is bright green.

Substitutions: This dish can be easily transformed into a chicken or beef stir-fry. Just cut ½ lb of meat into thin strips and marinate in ⅓ cup Soyaki for a few minutes or overnight, depending on your time. Substitute it for the tofu, and stir-fry ingredients in the same order.

Prep and cooking time: 15 minutes
Serves 4

Per serving: 193 calories, 12 g fat, 1 g saturated fat, 8 g protein, 13 g carbs, 3 g fiber, 7 g sugar, 716 mg sodium

Use GF teriyaki sauce, such as San-J or Seal Sama Teriyaki sauce, available at other grocers

A Betta Muffuletta

Where y'at! The muffuletta is one of the greatest sandwiches of all time but rarely seen outside New Orleans. More a meal than a sandwich, muffulettas are made with a crusty round Italian or French loaf, piled with provolone, salami-type meats, and a tasty olive mix. Our muffuletta is an individual-sized version of the classic. Use both hands and have a few extra napkins on hand. We won't claim we can pronounce "muffuletta" like a native New Orleanian, but we think this is the tastiest version outside of the Big Easy.

Country Style French Rolls (6-inch rounds) or any kind of crusty bread, preferably seeded

½ cup jarred Bruschetta

Sliced salami meats (mixed pack available containing a Mortadella, Genoa Salame, Coppa mix or a Genoa Salame and Provolone cheese mix)

Black Forest Healthy Smoked Ham (optional)

Sliced Provolone cheese (buy separately if you didn't get the mixed salami pack)

⅓ cup Green Olive Tapenade

1   Slice bread open.

2   From the bottom up, layer bruschetta, meats, cheese, and tapenade. Pile on meats and cheese according to your own likes.

3   Optional: for a more authentic preparation, wrap tightly in plastic wrap and then foil; place in fridge for a few hours, preferably with something placed on top to weigh it down. Leaving it for a few hours or even overnight allows the flavors to meld and the olive oil to soak into the bread.

Tip: *Jarred tapenades and bruschettas are often high in sodium. To reduce, sodium, omit them and add 1 piece jarred fire-roasted red pepper or a serving of roasted vegetables (page 186), lowering the sodium by more than half.*

Prep time: *5 minutes*
Serves 2

Per half-sandwich (using 2 oz meats and 1 slice cheese): 413 calories, 22 g fat, 5 g saturated fat, 17 g protein, 40 g carbs, 1 g fiber, 6 g sugar, 1665 mg sodium

It's a Wrap

Wraps are a versatile food. These cleverly packaged sandwiches are portable, easy to make, and really draw attention to the fillings rather than the bread. Tortillas and lavash are both great for wraps and are lower-carb options than traditional sandwich bread. The nice thing about preparing them is that the ingredient amounts are flexible—really no need to measure. Try the suggested wraps on the next few pages and then come up with your own custom versions! To pack for a lunch or a picnic, wrap tightly in aluminum foil or plastic wrap. Serve wraps with gourmet chips or fresh fruit.

Southwest Burrito

A flour tortilla wrapped around black beans, veggies, cheese, and salsa makes a perfect meal for anytime. You'll be surprised at the burst of flavor in this healthy, low-fat burrito.

1 large flour tortilla

3 heaping Tbsp canned black beans, drained

A few pieces of Oven Roasted Vegetables (page 186), Fire Roasted Red Peppers or Fire Roasted Yellow & Red Peppers

3 Tbsp Fancy Shredded Mexican Blend cheese

2 Tbsp Chunky Salsa

A few sprigs fresh cilantro

Slices of fresh avocado (optional)

Dollop of sour cream or yogurt (optional)

1   Place all ingredients down the center of the tortilla.

2   Roll tightly.

Prep time: *5 minutes*
Serves 1

Per serving: 211 calories, 4 g fat, 0 g saturated fat, 8 g protein, 36 g carbs, 3 g fiber, 2 g sugar, 633 mg sodium

Use brown rice tortilla

Turkey Artichoke Wrap

A classic turkey and Swiss combo takes on a flavorful twist by sharing the stage with red pepper and zesty pesto. This wrap is a quick and dependable standby for lunch or a picnic.

---

1 Lavash Bread or a large (burrito size) flour tortilla

2 slices Oven Roasted Turkey Breast deli meat

2 slices Swiss cheese

1 Tbsp refrigerated Grilled Artichoke & Parmesan Dip

Small handful of Organics Spring Mix

1 piece Fire Roasted Red Pepper

1   Spread artichoke dip on one half of the tortilla, avoiding edges. Place turkey and swiss cheese slices on the same half of the tortilla. Add red pepper and greens to the center.

2   Roll tightly.

Prep time: *5 minutes*
Serves 1

Per serving: 548 calories, 21 g fat, 11 g saturated fat, 37 g protein, 47 g carbs, 3 g fiber, 2 g sugar, 1035 mg sodium

 **G** *Gluten Free* *Use brown rice tortilla*

Vegetarian Hummus and Lentil Wrap

Packaged steamed lentils make this wrap a breeze. Tasty hummus, fresh greens, and creamy yogurt complete this delicious Middle Eastern combination. The sprouted wheat tortilla has a wonderful texture and holds together nicely, making this a good wrap to take on the road.

---

1 Sprouted Wheat Tortilla or Lavash Bread

3 Tbsp refrigerated Mediterranean Hummus or Eggplant Hummus

5 Tbsp refrigerated Steamed Lentils

¼ cup chopped tomatoes

1 small handful Micro Greens or Herb Salad Mix

2 Tbsp yogurt, such as Plain Cream Line Yogurt

1   Place lentils, hummus, tomatoes, and micro greens down the center of the tortilla; drizzle yogurt across lentils.

2   Roll tightly.

Prep time: *5 minutes*
Serves 1

Per serving: 429 calories, 8 g fat, 2 g saturated fat, 20 g protein, 74 g carbs, 11 g fiber, 8 g sugar, 648 mg sodium

G Gluten Free **V** Vegetarian

Use brown rice tortilla

Mozzarella and Basil Wrap

Basil, fresh mozzarella, pine nuts, and tomatoes create a fresh-from-the-garden taste. You can use pesto if you prefer, but we like the simple flavor of fresh basil in this wrap. In addition to contributing delicious taste, the basil acts as a moisture barrier, keeping your tortilla from getting soggy from the cheese.

---

1 large (burrito size) flour tortilla

3 Fresh Mozzarella Medallions or ¼-inch-thick slices Ovoline Fresh Mozzarella

4 fresh basil leaves

3 slices Roma tomatoes or other flavorful ripe tomato

1 Tbsp toasted pine nuts

1   Lay tortilla on a flat surface. Place basil leaves down the center of the tortilla. Add mozzarella, pine nuts, and tomato.

2   Roll tightly.

Prep time: 5 minutes
Serves 1

Per serving: 462 calories, 27 g fat, 11 g saturated fat, 23 g protein, 37 g carbs, 2 g fiber, 12 g sugar, 241 mg sodium

Use brown rice tortilla

Beer Suggestion

Asahi Super Dry Beer is a great beer choice for this dish. If you prefer to serve wine, try Now & Zen Alsace White, citrusy and crisp.

Soyaki Broiled Salmon

This is a twist on Teriyaki salmon. Dijon mustard adds a zing that will make ordinary Teriyaki sauces seem rather run-of-the-mill. If you've never used your broiler (yes, most ovens come with one built in), this is a good recipe to test it on. Cooking salmon under the high heat of a broiler will create a crusty top layer and lock in juices for a tender, flaky fillet. Prepare to be shocked at how easy this is! Pair with Peanutty Sesame Noodles (page 55) for a fabulous and fuss-free dinner party menu.

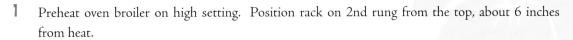

4 (6-oz) salmon fillets, preferably Wild Alaskan Salmon

½ cup Soyaki or Veri Veri Teriyaki

1 Tbsp Dijon mustard

2 green onions, chopped

1   Preheat oven broiler on high setting. Position rack on 2nd rung from the top, about 6 inches from heat.

2   Combine Soyaki and mustard. Pour over salmon and let it marinate for 10 minutes while oven is heating.

3   Place seasoned fillets on a foil-lined baking sheet, skin side down. Discard used marinade. Broil salmon for 6 minutes or until fish flakes easily.

4   Top with green onions.

Tip: *If you prefer to cook fish on the stove, heat a grill pan over medium heat. Cook 2-3 minutes on each side.*

Prep time: *5 minutes*
Hands-off cooking time: *6 minutes*
Serves 4

Per serving: *329 calories, 17 g fat, 3 g saturated fat, 37 g protein, 4 g carbs, 0 g fiber, 3 g sugar, 433 mg sodium*

 Use GF teriyaki sauce, such as San-J or Seal Sama Teriyaki sauce, available at other grocers

Honey Mustard Chicken

Sweet honey and tangy mustard meld in the oven to create a delicious glaze and dipping sauce. For best results, we recommend using fresh herbs. Serve with Orzo Pilaf (Page 185) or mashed potatoes.

4 chicken breasts or 6 thighs, bone-in or boneless

2 Tbsp olive oil

¼ cup flour

¼ tsp salt

⅛ tsp black pepper

½ cup honey

½ cup Dijon mustard

2 Tbsp chopped fresh basil

1   Preheat oven to 375° F.

2   Heat oil in a large sauté pan over medium-high heat. Mix flour with salt and pepper. Coat chicken pieces with seasoned flour, shaking off excess. Brown chicken on all sides. Transfer to a baking dish.

3   Mix honey, mustard, and basil. Pour sauce over chicken and bake for 30 minutes. Midway through the cooking, turn and baste chicken pieces once.

Substitution: *If you can get tarragon, substitute it for the basil. Called "King of Herbs" by the French, tarragon imparts a subtle licorice flavor that goes perfectly with honey and mustard.*

Prep time: *10 minutes*
Hands-off cooking time: *30 minutes*
Serves 4

Per serving: 379 calories, 13 g fat, 2 g saturated fat, 27 g protein, 43 g carbs, 0 g fiber, 32 g sugar, 715 mg sodium

 Gluten Free *Omit flour or use cornstarch*

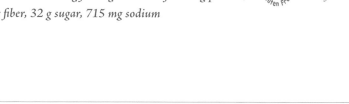

Pasta Puttanesca

This tasty dish has a risqué past. *Puttana* means "lady of the evening" and refers to ladies of easy virtue in Naples who tempted their customers with this meal. Traditional Puttanesca sauce is made with anchovies, but our version uses more readily available canned tuna. Think you don't like fish in your pasta sauce? Think again. Cooked in this dish, tuna contributes a warm nutty flavor, not fishy, and is a good source of omega-3 fatty acids.

---

1 (6-oz) can tuna, either in oil or water

2 cloves garlic, crushed, or 2 cubes frozen Crushed Garlic

Juice from half a lemon

1 lb penne pasta

2 tsp olive oil

⅓ cup Julienne Sliced Sun Dried Tomatoes

1 Tbsp capers

½ cup pitted Kalamata olives

½ tsp dried red pepper flakes

1 (28-oz) can diced tomatoes

¼ cup red table wine, such as "2 Buck Chuck"

¼ cup chopped parsley

2 Tbsp Shredded Parmesan Cheese

1 Drain tuna and mix with lemon juice and garlic. Set aside to marinate for 10-15 minutes while you cook the rest of the meal.

2 Cook pasta in salted water, according to package directions. Drain, reserving about ¼ cup pasta water to add to the sauce.

3 While pasta is cooking, heat olive oil in a medium saucepan. Add bruschetta, capers, olives, and red pepper to the saucepan and fry for 2-3 minutes. Add tomatoes and tuna (including marinade). Bring to a boil and cook for 5 minutes. Remove from heat.

4 Stir in parsley and reserved pasta water. Starch in the pasta water will help the sauce cling better to the pasta.

5 Pour sauce over pasta and garnish with Parmesan cheese.

Prep time: *10 minutes*
Hands-off cooking time: *20 minutes*
Serves 8

Per serving: 354 calories, 8 g fat, 2 g saturated fat, 19 g protein, 48 g carbs, 4 g fiber, 6 g sugar, 341 mg sodium

Chicken Marsala Casserole

Marsala sauce is a rich sauce with mushrooms, onions, and, of course, the key ingredient, Marsala wine, responsible for its unique flavor. This family-friendly casserole is a complete meal in one dish. Thanks to charbroiled Just Chicken and fresh tortellini, this dish is assembled quickly in one pan and goes straight into the oven. Serve with crusty Italian bread to soak up all the extra sauce!

3 cups (one 10-oz container) fresh refrigerated Cheese Tortellini, uncooked (do not use dry tortellini)

4 cups (1 lb) cooked chicken, or a 1-lb container refrigerated charbroiled Just Chicken, cut into ½-inch chunks

2 cups Shredded 3 Cheese Blend

4 cups (one 12-oz bag) fresh broccoli florets or frozen broccoli, thawed

1 (12-oz) jar Marsala Sauce (not to be confused with Masala Simmer Sauce) or make your own, below

1 ½ cups chicken broth

1 Preheat oven to 350° F.

2 Place fresh tortellini in an ungreased 9 x 13-inch casserole dish in a single layer. Top evenly with chicken chunks, shredded cheese, and broccoli florets, in that order.

3 Combine Marsala sauce and chicken broth in a bowl and pour over casserole.

4 Cover with a lid or foil and bake for 30 minutes.

Prep time: 5 minutes
Hands-off cooking time: 30 minutes
Serves 8

Per serving: 448 calories, 15 g fat, 7 g saturated fat, 36 g protein, 34 g carbs, 3 g fiber, 4 g sugar, 709 mg sodium

Homemade Marsala Sauce

2 Tbsp olive oil

1 onion, diced

2 cloves garlic, crushed, or 2 cubes frozen Crushed Garlic

1 (8-10 oz) pkg white mushrooms, sliced

¼ cup flour

1 ½ cups chicken broth

¾ cup Marsala wine

¼ cup chopped fresh parsley (optional)

1 In a sauce pan over high heat, sauté onions in oil until tender.

2 Add garlic and mushrooms; cook and stir for additional 2-3 minutes until mushrooms are cooked but plump.

3 Whisk in flour, sautéing for additional 1 minute. Add Marsala wine and broth, cooking until sauce thickens slightly. Stir in parsley.

Note: *Making your own Marsala sauce reduces the sodium to 450 mg per serving.*

Wine Suggestion:

Try Chateau Ste. Michelle Chardonnay, a bright and rich food-friendly Chardonnay, crisp with citrus and tropical flavors.

Comfy Chicken Pot Pie

No matter where you go, there's nothing like the smell and warmth of chicken pot pie to bring you back home and soothe your soul. Here is an easy version of the all-time comfort food. If you can't find pie crusts, top the filling with Easy Cheesy Drop Biscuits (recipe below) instead.

3 cups cooked chicken, such as refrigerated charbroiled Just Chicken, cubed

2 Tbsp butter

2 Tbsp flour

1 cup milk

1 cup chicken broth

1 (16-oz) pkg frozen Vegetable Melange (about 3 cups), or other vegetable mix, thawed

1 frozen pie crust or homemade Easy Cheesy Biscuits (recipe below)

Salt and pepper to taste

1 Preheat oven to 350° F. Defrost pie crusts according to package instructions.

2 Melt butter in a medium pot over medium-high heat. Add flour and cook for 2 minutes, stirring frequently. Add milk and broth. Simmer 5 minutes or until sauce is thickened and coats the back of a spoon.

3 Stir in chicken and vegetables, coating all pieces evenly. Season with salt and pepper to taste.

4 Line 9-inch pie pan with 1 pie crust. Pour chicken mixture into 9-inch pie pan. Top with crust and crimp edges to seal around edge of pan. If using biscuits, drop by spoonfuls on top of filling.

5 Place pie on a baking sheet to catch any drippings. Bake for 30 minutes or until top is golden brown.

Easy Cheesy Drop Biscuits

2 cups Buttermilk Pancake Mix

1 ½ Tbsp melted butter

⅔ cup milk

½ cup shredded cheddar cheese

1 Mix pancake mix, butter, and milk with a fork until just combined. Fold in cheese. Drop dough by heaping spoonfuls onto chicken mixture.

Prep time: 15 minutes
Hands-off cooking time: 30 minutes
Serves 6

Per serving: 618 calories, 26 g fat, 8 g saturated fat, 33 g protein, 46 g carbs, 5 g fiber, 9 g sugar, 503 mg sodium

Dress to Impress Lobster Ravioli

Here's an easy way to get the gourmet flavor of lobster without having to get your hands messy cracking claws. We dress the ravioli with a creamy pink sauce that doesn't overpower the delicate taste of lobster. Serve with a simple side of steamed broccolini (baby broccoli).

2 (9-oz) pkg refrigerated Lobster Ravioli

1 cup Organic Vodka Sauce or marinara

1 cup heavy whipping cream or whole milk

2 Tbsp sliced fresh basil

2 Tbsp grated Parmesan cheese

1   Cook lobster ravioli according to package directions. Drain.

2   Heat vodka sauce and cream in a medium saucepan over medium heat, stirring to combine. Boil for 5 minutes until sauce is slightly thickened.

3   Pour sauce over ravioli. Garnish with basil and Parmesan cheese.

Prep and cooking time: *10 minutes*
Serves 5

Per serving: 318 calories, 15 g fat, 3 g saturated fat, 6 g protein, 35 g carbs, 4 g fiber, 11 g sugar, 963 mg sodium

160

Wine Suggestion:

A smooth and buttery Chardonnay, such as **La Crema Chardonnay**, won't overpower the delicate lobster flavors and will balance the cream sauce.

Beer Suggestion:

Beer goes great with spicy food, and **Trader Joe's Vienna Style Lager** has the balanced sweetness for the spice of this dish.

Tex-Mex Fajitas

Fajitas may have been what made Tex-Mex cuisine famous – grilled meats served in corn or flour tortillas with a variety of condiments. Who among us hasn't turned our heads in restaurants to admire fajita meat sizzling loudly on a hot skillet? Recreate this exciting restaurant flavor effortlessly using pre-marinated meats and pre-sliced fajitas vegetables. Simply lay out the condiments and let each person assemble his or her own fajita.

1 (2-lb) pkg premarinated Carne Asada Autentica or Pollo Asado Autentico

1 onion, sliced

2 bell peppers of any color, sliced

12 small corn or flour tortillas

Optional toppings:

Southwest Salsa

Refrigerated Avocado's Number Guacamole

Fancy Shredded Mexican Blend cheese

Sour cream

1 Heat a grill pan or skillet over medium-high heat. Cook beef or chicken to desired doneness. Remove meat from pan and cover with foil. Allow to rest for 10 minutes.

2 Meanwhile, grill vegetables in the same pan. The vegetables will be flavored with fajita seasonings from the meat. Cook for 5 minutes; vegetables should be slightly crisp.

3 Slice meat diagonally into long strips. Place grilled vegetables on serving platter and arrange meat slices on top.

4 Serve with tortillas and tray of condiments.

Prep and cooking time: *15 minutes*
Serves 6 amigos

Per serving: 291 calories, 11 g fat, 3 g saturated fat, 30 g protein, 25 g carbs, 15 g fiber, 2 g sugar, 702 mg sodium

Garlic & Herb Chicken Roast

Picking up a rotisserie chicken at the grocery store is so easy these days that roasting a chicken at home seems like a lost art. But if you're craving that honest-to-goodness home-baked flavor or want full control over the quality of the chicken you eat, you're about to find out how easy it is to roast chicken at home.

---

1 (5-7 lb) whole chicken

2 tsp salt

1 tsp black pepper

1 (1-oz) pkg Poultry Blend fresh herbs, or make your own blend of rosemary, thyme, sage (1-2 sprigs of each fresh, or 1 tsp of each dried)

1 lemon, cut in half

1 entire bulb of garlic, cut in half across all the cloves

1 Tbsp unsalted butter, melted, or olive oil

Vegetables such as potatoes, parsnips, carrots, and onions, quartered or cut in 1 ½-inch pieces (optional)

1 Preheat oven to 425° F.

2 Remove giblets from cavity of chicken. Rinse chicken inside and out, and then pat dry with paper towels. This will help the butter stick better to the skin.

3 Stuff cavity with 1 tsp salt, ½ tsp pepper, herbs, lemon, garlic, and onion. Tie legs together with string. Fold wings under the bird to prevent them from burning.

4 Rub melted butter all over chicken. Sprinkle remaining salt and pepper over entire chicken.

5 Put vegetables in baking dish and place chicken on top. The vegetables act as a cooking rack for the chicken and get flavored in delicious chicken juices with no effort.

6 Cook for 1 ½ hours, until juices run clear when thigh is pierced with a knife or thermometer reads 170° F. If you're cooking a smaller chicken, start checking for doneness after 1 hour.

7 Remove chicken from heat. Cover with foil and allow to rest for 20 minutes.

Prep time: *10 minutes*

Hands-off cooking time: *60-90 minutes (roughly 15 minutes per pound of chicken)*

Serves 6; *use leftovers in place of Just Chicken in many of our recipes!*

Per 4 oz serving of white meat: 110 calories, 2.5 g fat, 0.5 g saturated fat, 23 g protein, 0 g carbs, 0 g fiber, 0 g sugar, 180 mg sodium

Per 4 oz serving of dark meat: 207 calories, 11 g fat, 3 g saturated fat, 26 g protein, 2 g carbs, 0 g fiber, 0 g sugar, 410 mg sodium

Wine Suggestion:

Try a red wine low in tannin such as a Pinot Noir, or perhaps a versatile red blend such as *Chariot Gypsy*, a favorite food-friendly wine at a bargain price.

Eggplant Parmesan Pasta

This casual dish was invented by my 2-year-old toddler who loves stirring food together. He took his bowl of cut-up eggplant parmesan and pasta and stirred away in between each bite. Little did he know he had recreated Pasta alla Norma, a traditional dish widely popular in Sicily. We adults found it was a nice way to spread the yummy gooey sauce, cheese, and eggplant throughout the pasta. Serve it in rustic pasta bowls, no knives required. Keep an extra Eggplant Parmesan package in the freezer for a quick weeknight meal.

1 (24-oz) pkg refrigerated Roasted Eggplant Parmesan (frozen options also available, but require extra sauce and cheese)

3 cups farfalle or pasta of your choice

1 Tbsp chopped fresh basil or parsley

1   Cook pasta according to package directions. Drain.

2   While pasta is cooking, heat eggplant parmesan according to package directions. Cut eggplant into bite-size pieces. Do not discard any sauce or cheese – they will coat the pasta with great flavor.

3   Stir together pasta and eggplant. Garnish with basil.

Prep time: *5 minutes*
Hands-off cooking time: *10 minutes*
Serves 4

Per serving: 578 calories, 19 g fat, 7 g saturated fat, 23 g protein, 75 g carbs, 5 g fiber, 4 g sugar, 555 mg sodium

Calamari Brodetto

Sicilian-inspired brodetto is a rich stew, typically based on seafood. In this recipe, tender calamari rings are combined with the layered flavors of garlic, lemon, capers, tomato, and olives. Serve with crusty Italian bread on the side, or place a slice of bread on a plate and ladle the stew over it. For a more soup-like consistency, substitute an equivalent amount of Italian Tortellini with Mushrooms for the grains and pasta.

2 cups frozen calamari rings, thawed

2 cups chicken broth

2 cups water

1 Tbsp extra virgin olive oil

1 cup Harvest Grains Blend

1 cup Trottole (large spiral pasta) or any other large pasta

4 pieces sun dried tomatoes, cut into small pieces

10 pitted Kalamata olives

1 Tbsp capers, drained

¾ cup refrigerated Fresh Bruschetta Sauce

2 Tbsp lemon juice (juice of ½ lemon)

1   Add broth, water, and olive oil to a medium pot and bring to a boil. Add pasta and grain blend; cook for 12 minutes. The dish will thicken to a nice stew consistency as it cooks

2   Add tomatoes, olives, capers and return to a boil.

3   Add calamari rings, bruschetta sauce, and lemon juice. Cook for an additional 2-3 minutes or until pasta is *al dente*. Don't overcook the calamari rings or they will become rubbery.

Prep and cooking time: *15-20 minutes*
Serves 4

Per serving: 422 calories, 11 g fat, 1 g saturated fat, 19 g protein, 62 g carbs, 4 g fiber, 7 g sugar, 559 mg sodium

Wine Suggestion:

For a rich brodetto or bouillabaisse, try a fresh and fruity rosé (also called a blush), such as the French **La Ferme Julien Rosé**.

Shredded Pork Enchiladas Verde

Salsa verde is a "green" mild salsa made with tomatillos, which are firmer than tomatoes and taste like tangy lemons. We use it as the base for these enchiladas filled with tender ready-to-eat carnitas, a slow-cooked braised pork. Substitute black beans for a vegetarian version.

1 (12-oz) pkg refrigerated Traditional Carnitas, shredded (about 2 cups)

12 corn tortillas (taco size, about 6 inches across)

2 Tbsp canola oil

1 ½ (12-oz) jars Salsa Verde

1 ½ cups sour cream

1 cup grated pecorino romano cheese

1 cup Very American Salad (blend of iceberg, romaine, red cabbage), thinly sliced

1 cup frozen Roasted Corn, thawed

¼ cup cilantro, chopped

1   Preheat oven to 350° F.

2   Pour oil into a frying pan just bigger than tortillas and heat over medium heat. Using tongs, toast tortillas for 3-5 seconds on each side, only until they become limp.

3   Combine ½ cup salsa, 1 cup sour cream, and cilantro, reserving remaining sour cream and some cilantro for garnish.

4   To assemble enchiladas, place 2 heaping Tbsp pork, 2 Tbsp sour cream mixture, and 1 Tbsp cheese on each tortilla. Roll up enchiladas and place seam side down in a buttered 9 x 13-inch pan.

5   Bake for 10 minutes, just long enough for cheeses to melt.

6   Pour remaining salsa on top. Garnish with salad, corn, sour cream, and cilantro.

Prep time: *20 minutes*
Hands-off cooking time: *10 minutes*
Serves 6

Per serving: 525 calories, 29 g fat, 13 g saturated fat, 21 g protein, 36 g carbs, 3 g fiber, 7 g sugar, 1281 mg sodium

Wine Suggestion:

For a regional pairing go with a Malbec, the dark and robust wine from Argentina. Closer to home, **Robert Hall Syrah** combines dark berry and smoky notes with a rich finish, for a lively wine that pairs well with grilled steak and meats.

Chimichurri Grill

Chimichurri sauce is to Argentina what ketchup is to the U.S. Chimichurri is a delicious blend of olive oil, vinegar, herbs, and spices and is traditionally served over grilled meats. It is ultra versatile – use it as a marinade, a relish, or a bread dipper. The lively sauce will make your steaks burst with the flavors of a fresh herb garden.

4 steaks (rib-eye or tenderloin are good choices)

4 sausages of your choice, such as Fully-Cooked Garlic & Herb Chicken Sausages

2 Tbsp Steak & Chop Grill & Broil seasoning

¼ cup soy sauce

¼ cup olive oil

½ cup refrigerated Chimichurri Sauce, plus extra for dipping, or make your own, recipe below (optional)

1 Combine steak seasoning, soy sauce, and olive oil in a bowl or Ziploc bag. Add steaks and marinate for at least 30 minutes and up to overnight. Discard used marinade.

2 Grill steaks and sausage to desired doneness; a grill pan on the stove works as nicely as an outdoor grill.

3 Top with generous spoonfuls of Chimichurri sauce. We recommend serving additional Chimichurri sauce in a bowl.

Prep time: *5 minutes*
Cooking time: *10 minutes*
Serves 8

Chimichurri Sauce

½ cup olive oil

½ cup chopped fresh parsley

½ cup chopped fresh cilantro

1 tsp dried oregano

3 cloves garlic, crushed, or 3 cubes frozen Crushed Garlic

½ tsp red pepper flakes

½ tsp salt

¼ cup red wine vinegar

1 Purée all ingredients in a food processor, or mix together for a more rustic version (chop herbs more finely if skipping the processor).

Per serving: 398 calories, 25 g fat, 9 g saturated fat, 25 g protein, 0 g carbs, 1 g fiber, 2 g sugar, 393 mg sodium

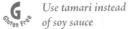 *Use tamari instead of soy sauce*

Simple Sides

Olive-Stuffed Bread

A few minutes of work yields a rustic yet sophisticated crusty loaf with the salty surprise of olives inside. It's a nice bread to enjoy warm with cheese, alongside an appetizer, or with a full meal.

1 (1-lb) bag refrigerated dough

½ cup Green Olive Tapenade or your favorite bruschetta or tapenade

1   Preheat oven to 425° F.

2   On a floured surface, roll dough (or stretch out with hands) so it is about 6 x 15 inches. Spoon tapenade down the center lengthwise, except for the last inch at each end. Pull up sides of bread and firmly pinch a seam down the center, sealing in bruschetta.

3   Place seam-side down on a pizza stone (preferred method) or an oiled baking sheet and bake for 30-35 minutes, or until crust is golden brown.

4   Slice loaf into 1-inch pieces and serve warm.

Prep time: 5 minutes
Hands-off cooking time: 30 minutes
Serves 8

Per serving: 150 calories, 4 g fat, 0 g saturated fat, 3 g protein, 25 g carbs, 1 g fiber, 0 g sugar, 660 mg sodium

Vegetarian

Wilted Spinach with Attitude

It's easy to eat your spinach when it's this tasty and easy to make. As a child, I remember struggling to force down cafeteria-style over-cooked spinach drowning in vinegar – it's no wonder kids hated spinach back then. This version is nothing like that. Fresh spinach is cooked quickly until just wilted, preserving a vibrant green color and fresh flavor.

2 (6-oz) bags baby spinach

1 Tbsp olive oil

3 cloves garlic, crushed, or 3 cubes frozen Crushed Garlic

¼ cup water

½ tsp salt

Juice from half a lemon (optional)

1   Heat olive oil in a large pan over medium-high heat. Add garlic and fry for 30 seconds, being careful not to let the garlic brown. Garlic burns easily and tastes bitter when browned.

2   Add spinach, water, and salt. Cover and cook for 2 minutes. Lift cover and stir spinach with tongs, tossing leaves so that all the spinach wilts evenly.

3   As soon as all leaves are wilted, remove from heat. Squeeze half a lemon over spinach and mix. Serve immediately.

Prep and cooking time: *5 minutes*
Serves 4

Per serving: 54 calories, 4 g fat, 1 g saturated fat, 3 g protein,
4 g carbs, 2 g fiber, 0 g sugar, 357 mg sodium

G
Gluten Free

Vegetarian

Wild about Brown Rice Pilaf

The pre-packaged brown rice mixture combines the interesting textures and flavors of long grain brown rice, black barley, and Daikon radish seeds. Brown rice never had such unique company. Toasting the rice keeps the rice grains separated and makes a fluffy pilaf. Wild mushrooms add wonderful flavor and texture to this dish. Wild mushrooms grow in flushes, but with dried wild mushrooms, you can enjoy their flavor year round.

---

1 cup Brown Rice Medley

1 tsp olive oil

½ cup chopped onion or bagged Freshly Diced Onion

2 cups chicken or vegetable broth

1 (1-oz) pkg dried Mixed Wild Mushrooms, soaked in ½ cup hot water and chopped (keep water)

1 Tbsp fresh parsley, chopped

1 Heat olive oil in a medium pot over medium-high heat. Add onions and cook for 5 minutes. Stir in rice; toast for a few minutes, stirring frequently.

2 Pour in chicken broth and mushrooms including water; heat to boiling. Reduce heat to simmer and cook, covered, for 35 minutes.

3 Remove from heat and stir in parsley. Cover and let stand 10 minutes longer. Fluff with a fork before serving.

Prep time: *10 minutes*
Hands-off cooking time: *35 minutes*
Serves 4

Per serving: 230 calories, 4 g fat, 1 g saturated fat, 9 g protein, 40 g carbs, 8 g fiber, 1 g sugar, 278 mg sodium

Use gluten-free broth and plain brown rice (Brown Rice Medley contains barley)

Balsamic Green Beans

Shallots and balsamic vinaigrette are a delicious sauce duo, especially in this green bean and potato side dish.

1 lb green beans, ends trimmed

1 Tbsp butter

1 Tbsp extra virgin olive oil

2 shallots, minced (about 2 Tbsp)

1 cup Baby Dutch Yellow Potatoes, unpeeled, cut into ½-inch pieces

1 cup chicken or vegetable broth

2 Tbsp Balsamic Vinaigrette dressing

1 Tbsp cornstarch dissolved in 2 Tbsp hot water

1   Put olive oil and butter in a large skillet on medium high heat. When butter melts, add shallots and potatoes, sautéing for about 5 minutes.

2   Add broth, green beans, and balsamic vinaigrette. Stir well, bring to a simmer, then turn heat to medium-low and cover with a lid for about 8 minutes.

3   Moving the green beans slightly to one side to expose a section of the broth, add cornstarch and stir quickly to incorporate and form a thickened sauce. Cook for an additional 4 minutes and serve.

Prep and cooking time: *25 minutes*
Serves 6

Per serving: 101 calories, 5 g fat, 2 g saturated fat, 3 g protein, 12 g carbs, 3 g fiber, 2 g sugar, 146 mg sodium

Choose gluten-free broth

Cooking with All Things Trader Joe's

Orzo Pilaf

Pressed for time? Try orzo instead of rice. It cooks up faster and is just as versatile. Trader Joe's new Harvest Grains Blend combines orzo, baby garbanzo beans, and red quinoa for unexpected colors and textures.

---

1 ¼ cups Harvest Grains Blend (half the package)

2 tsp olive oil

½ cup chopped onion or bagged Freshly Diced Onion

½ cup chopped red bell pepper

1 ¾ cups chicken or vegetable broth

2 Tbsp grated Parmesan cheese

1   Heat olive oil in a medium pot over medium-high heat. Add onions and bell pepper and cook for 5 minutes. Stir in orzo blend and toast for a few minutes, stirring frequently.

2   Pour in chicken broth and heat to boiling. Reduce heat to simmer and cook, covered, for 10 minutes.

3   Stir in Parmesan cheese. Serve immediately.

Prep time: *10 minutes*
Hands-off cooking time: *10 minutes*
Serves 4

Per serving: 264 calories, 4 g fat, 1 g saturated fat, 10 g protein, 46 g carbs, 3 g fiber, 4 g sugar, 282 mg sodium

Oven Roasted Vegetables with Rosemary

Your kitchen is going to smell great as you roast vegetables with garlic and fresh rosemary. This healthy selection of squash, sweet potato, and red pepper is a nice accompaniment to nearly any entrée. The conveniently prepped bagged vegetables make this dish a breeze without all the peeling and chopping. Keep leftovers for use in wraps or sandwiches the next day!

2 zucchini, sliced thinly lengthwise (¼-inch thick or less)

1 cup cut butternut squash (available bagged)

1 cup cut yams (available bagged)

1 red bell pepper, quartered, with seeds and pith removed

6-8 garlic cloves, peeled

3 Tbsp extra virgin olive oil

½ tsp salt

¼ tsp pepper

A few sprigs fresh rosemary

1   Preheat oven to 425° F.

2   Toss vegetables with olive oil, salt, and pepper, thoroughly coating all vegetables.

3   Place vegetables in a single layer in a 9 x 13-inch roasting/baking pan. Make sure red peppers are "cut side down." Place pan in the oven and roast uncovered for 20 minutes.

4   Add rosemary and roast for an additional 10-15 minutes or until veggies look done.

Prep time: *10 minutes*
Hands-off cooking time: *35 minutes*
Serves 6

Per serving: 122 calories, 7 g fat, 1 g saturated fat, 2 g protein, 15 g carbs, 3 g fiber, 3 g sugar, 178 mg sodium

Curried Couscous with Almonds

Couscous, originally from Morocco, is a staple throughout Africa, much the same way rice is in Asia. Made of tiny pasta grains, couscous is especially popular because it cooks so quickly – simply soak in boiling water for 5 minutes and it's ready. Flavor couscous with virtually any vegetable, herb, spice, or fruit you can think of. The possibilities are limitless.

1 cup Whole Wheat Couscous

¼ cup Thai Yellow Curry Sauce

1 cup chicken or vegetable broth

½ cup slivered almonds

¼ cup sliced green onions

1 Heat curry sauce and chicken broth in a medium-sized saucepan. When mixture comes to a boil, stir in couscous. Cover pan and remove from heat. Let stand 5 minutes covered.

2 Fluff couscous with a fork. Stir in almonds and green onions.

Variation: Try using 1 teaspoon Spanish Saffron instead of curry sauce. You can also add a variety of dried fruit, including raisins, currants, apricots, or cranberries. Try other nuts too, such as pine nuts or walnuts.

Prep and cooking time: *10 minutes*
Serves 4

Per serving: 277 calories, 10 g fat, 1 g saturated fat, 10 g protein, 39 g carbs, 7 g fiber, 5 g sugar, 378 mg sodium

Green Garbanzo Salad

This simple salad is a versatile starter or side. Green garbanzos are sure to be a conversation starter, as are the tiny mozzarella balls. The trick to making this easy salad is cooking the garbanzos in salted water; be generous with the salt, just like when you're cooking pasta. That way there will be flavor throughout the beans, not just on the outside from the dressing.

2 cups frozen Green Garbanzos or shelled edamame

2 tsp salt to flavor boiling water

½ cup Perlini Super Tiny Fresh Mozzarella balls, or cut your own mozzarella

¼ cup diced red onion

½ tsp crushed garlic, or 1 cube frozen Crushed Garlic

¼ cup Tuscan Italian Dressing or homemade Lemon Basil Vinaigrette (recipe below)

1 Cook garbanzo beans in salted water. Drain.

2 Combine all vegetables in a large bowl. Pour vinaigrette over salad, add mozzarella balls, and toss gently.

3 Garnish with fresh basil.

Lemon Basil Vinaigrette

1 Tbsp fresh lemon juice

¼ tsp Dijon mustard

3 Tbsp extra virgin olive oil

2 tsp fresh basil, chopped

Pinch sugar or ¼ tsp honey

1 Combine lemon juice and mustard. Drizzle in olive oil and whisk until combined. Add basil and sugar and stir.

Prep time: *10 minutes*
Hands-off cooking time: *10 minutes*
Serves 4

Per serving: 213 calories, 15 g fat, 3 g saturated fat, 6 g protein, 14 g carbs, 4 g fiber, 5 g sugar, 183 mg sodium

It's Easy Bein' Green Veggie Gratin

Reminiscent of Grandma's green bean casserole, but not those mushy, salty, canned green beans. Instead, we use a fresh frozen blend of broccoli, edamame, asparagus, spinach, and green beans. They cook up beautifully in a light cheesy sauce and are topped with crunchy fried onion pieces. If you don't like fried onions, you can make an easy breadcrumb topping (recipe below).

---

1 (1-lb) bag frozen Organic Greens with Envy, thawed, or plain green beans, or your own mixture of greens

½ cup Alfredo Pasta Sauce

½ cup milk

½ cup Fried Onion Pieces or Easy Breadcrumb Topping (recipe below)

1　Preheat oven to 375° F.

2　Mix Alfredo sauce with milk until well blended. Add vegetables and toss to coat.

3　Pour vegetable mixture into a buttered baking dish. Cover dish with foil and bake for 20 minutes.

4　Remove foil and sprinkle gratin with fried onions. Bake uncovered for 10 minutes.

Easy Breadcrumb Topping

¼ cup breadcrumbs

¼ cup Parmesan cheese

1 Tbsp melted butter

1　Mix until combined and sprinkle evenly on veggies.

Prep time: 5 minutes
Hands-off cooking time: 30 minutes
Serves 6

Per serving: 124 calories, 7 g fat, 3 g saturated fat, 6 g protein, 10 g carbs, 3 g fiber, 1 g sugar, 210 mg sodium

Pan-Toasted Brussels Sprouts

Who hasn't eaten a Brussels sprout and pretended to be a giant eating an entire head of cabbage in one bite? Chicken broth steams and flavors the Brussels sprouts, making them ready in a hurry in this fabulous pan-fried recipe. The Guinness record for eating Brussels sprouts is 44 in one minute. Try our recipe and you might be a contender.

1 (12-oz) pkg Brussels sprouts

2 tsp olive oil or butter

½ cup chicken or vegetable broth

Grated or shredded Parmesan cheese (optional)

1 Heat olive oil in saucepan over medium heat.

2 Cut Brussels sprouts in half. Place them cut-side down in hot pan. Add chicken broth. When broth comes to a boil, cover and cook for 5 minutes.

3 Remove lid and continue to cook until broth evaporates and Brussels sprouts are browned.

4 Remove from heat and sprinkle with Parmesan cheese.

Prep and cooking time: *10 minutes*
Serves 4

Per serving: 63 calories, 3 g fat, 0 g saturated fat, 2 g protein, 6 g carbs, 3 g fiber, 2 g sugar, 97 mg sodium

Choose gluten-free broth

Raita (Cucumber Yogurt Dip)

Raita is a traditional accompaniment to spicy and very flavorful Indian and Middle Eastern dishes. Cucumber, yogurt, and mint are such a refreshing and cooling combination. The raisins are a nice balance to both the taste and texture of this dish. Serve this dish as an appetizer with cut pita triangles or pita chips, or as a side dish to any Indian or Middle Eastern meal.

---

2 cups plain yogurt, such as Plain Cream Line Yogurt or Greek Style Plain Yogurt

½ cup raisins (we use Organic Thompson Seedless Raisins)

1 cup peeled and finely diced cucumber (2 Persian cucumbers or 1 medium cucumber)

2 Tbsp finely chopped fresh mint or 2 tsp dried mint

¼ tsp salt

1   Mix all ingredients in a serving bowl and serve right away.

2   Raita can be chilled in the fridge for 1 or 2 hours if prepared ahead of time, but it doesn't keep well overnight since the raisins swell.

Prep time: *10 minutes*
Serves 6

Per serving: 97 calories, 3 g fat, 2 g saturated fat, 3 g protein, 14 g carbs, 1 g fiber, 5 g sugar, 129 mg sodium

Delicious Desserts
& Daring Drinks

Honey, I Ate the Chocolate Bread Pudding

Cold vanilla ice cream melting on warm bread pudding is one of those feel-good dessert combinations. And this recipe makes a happy cook as well. There's no melting butter, no measuring ingredients… just toss it all in and bake. Trader Joe's also makes Whole Wheat Orange or White Orange versions of the bread used in this recipe, which can be substituted. We like to justify our chocolate indulgences by claiming that it's healthy since we use whole wheat! Serve warm with vanilla ice cream. Or if you really want to be indulgent (we encourage it), serve with chocolate ice cream.

½ loaf (8 slices) Whole Wheat Honey Bread

1 ½ cups Brownie Truffle Baking Mix (just the dry mix, don't add anything else)

2 ½ cups whole milk

1   Cut crusts off bread slices. Cube bread into ½-inch by ½-inch pieces. Toss diced bread in an 8 x 8-inch lightly greased or buttered baking pan and arrange so pan is filled evenly.

2   Combine milk and brownie mix. Stir well for a minute until dissolved. Pour brownie mixture over diced bread. Lightly press down on bread pieces so that they are thoroughly soaked through with brownie liquid.

3   Set pan aside while you preheat oven to 350° F, perhaps 10 minutes or so. This extra time will give the bread time to soak further. Cover pan tightly with foil and bake for 30 minutes.

4   When done, remove pan from oven and let it cool for 15 minutes, allowing bread pudding to set. Serve warm.

Prep time: *5-10 minutes*
Hands-off cooking time: *30 minutes*
Serves 9

Per serving: 272 calories, 5 g fat, 3 g saturated fat, 7 g protein, 56 g carbs, 4 g fiber, 29 g sugar, 201 mg sodium

Frozen Tiramisu

If you love tiramisu but don't have the time to make it, here is a luscious frozen version that can be assembled in minutes and requires no pastry skills. Even better, it doesn't use raw eggs like the traditional version. Ice cream aficionados say they like our version better than the traditional one.

½ gallon vanilla ice cream or gelato

½ cup strong coffee (instant is fine: mix 1 Tbsp instant coffee into ½ cup hot water)

¼ cup white or dark rum

1 box Soft Lady Fingers (24 cookies)

1 oz bittersweet chocolate such as Valrhona 71% Cacao bar, coarsely grated

Cocoa powder or ground cinnamon (optional)

1 Soften ice cream in microwave for 1 minute, using the defrost setting. Or, let ice cream soften on your countertop for 20 minutes.

2 Meanwhile, mix coffee and rum in a shallow bowl. Working with 1-2 ladyfingers at a time, soak ladyfingers in coffee mixture for 2-3 seconds on each side and then place into freezer-safe pan, making an even layer. (An 8 x 8-inch square pan works well for this recipe. 12 ladyfingers, or two rows of 6 cookies, cover the bottom perfectly.)

3 Stir softened ice cream until smooth. Pour half the ice cream into pan and spread evenly.

4 Place another layer of soaked ladyfingers (2 rows of 6 cookies) on top of ice cream. Cover ladyfingers with remaining ice cream. Cover top layer with plastic wrap and freeze tiramisu for at least 4 hours.

5 When ready to serve, remove plastic wrap and discard. Garnish with grated chocolate, cocoa powder, and ground cinnamon.

Variation: *If you love the flavor of coffee, try using coffee ice cream instead of vanilla ice cream.*

Prep time: *15 minutes (not including thawing)*
Serves 8

Per serving: 367 calories, 17 g fat, 10 g saturated fat, 6 g protein, *45 g carbs, 1 g fiber, 38 g sugar, 133 mg sodium*

Sangria

Sangria is a delicious and easy Spanish wine and fruit punch, traditionally made with Bordeaux wine although the idea has been adapted to all kinds of wines and fruits. Even if you have friends who aren't "wine people," there's a good chance they'll like sangria! Serve sangria in a pitcher as a party drink, a summertime punch, or as a perfect accompaniment to our Seafood Paella (page 91).

1 bottle red wine, like Picket Fence Pinot Noir

1 lime, cut in thin slices

1 orange, cut in thin slices

1 apple, cut in thin slices

1 cup cold French Market Lemonade or other fizzy lemon/lime soda

1   Combine wine and fruits in a clear glass pitcher, and place in fridge for at least one hour.

2   Add lemonade or soda just before serving.

Prep time: *10 minutes*
Serves 4

Per serving: 229 calories, 0 g fat, 0 g saturated fat, 1 g protein, 25 g carbs, 2 g fiber, 8 g sugar, 7 mg sodium

One Bowl Peach & Blueberry Cobbler

This may be the easiest cobbler you can make. Simply throw all the ingredients in an oven-safe dish and top with any fruit you have on hand. The result is warm fruit comfortably nestled in soft pillows of dough. Serve with whipped cream or a scoop of vanilla ice cream.

1 cup Buttermilk Pancake Mix

¼ cup butter, melted

½ cup sugar

½ cup milk

3 cups sliced peaches (fresh, frozen, or canned, such as jarred Peaches in Light Syrup) drained and thawed if using frozen

½ cup blueberries, fresh or frozen (not drained and thawed)

¼ tsp ground cinnamon (optional)

1   Preheat oven to 375° F.

2   Select an 8 x 8-inch square ovenproof dish or a glass 9-inch pie plate for the cobbler. (If you're feeding a crowd, double the recipe and use a 9 x13-inch baking dish.) Melt butter right in the baking dish and use it as a mixing bowl.

3   Add pancake mix, sugar, and milk to melted butter. Stir with a fork until just combined. Batter will be lumpy – do not over mix.

4   Scatter peaches and blueberries evenly over batter. Lightly sprinkle cinnamon evenly on top.

5   Bake for 30 minutes or until light golden brown.

Variations: *Use apples, pears, plums, or mixed berries. Frozen and canned fruit work just as well as fresh fruit in this recipe, but be sure to thaw and drain first.*

Prep time: *5 minutes*
Hands-off cooking time: *30 minutes*
Serves 4

Per serving: 389 calories, 14 g fat, 8 g saturated fat, 6 g protein, 63 g carbs, 3 g fiber, 42 g sugar, 469 mg sodium

Saffron Ice Cream

Something magical happens when saffron and vanilla come together. This ice cream is a takeoff of a classic Persian ice cream and is an unusual use for Trader Joe's Spanish Saffron. It's a pretty and uniquely-flavored ice cream that you'll get asked for again and again.

1 pint (2 cups) vanilla ice cream

1 tsp Spanish Saffron

2 Tbsp raw pistachio nutmeats, crushed or chopped coarsely. Reserve a few whole pistachios as topping.

1   Leave ice cream container out until ice cream is just softened enough to stir (or microwave on defrost setting in 10 second intervals).

2   Place saffron threads in a small cup; add 2 Tbsp water and let sit for 5 minutes, stirring a little with the back of a knife or your finger until the color and flavor are released.

3   Leaving ice cream in its container, pour saffron onto ice cream and stir until color is a uniform light "saffron yellow" (don't worry if saffron threads are visible; that is okay). Add chopped pistachios and stir.

4   Put lid back on and re-freeze until ice cream sets again.

5   When you serve it, top ice cream with more pistachios.

Note: *You won't find rose water at Trader Joe's, but if you live near a Middle Eastern grocery, pick up a bottle of distilled rose water. Mix 2 Tbsp rose water into the ice cream along with the saffron and you will get a very authentic flavor.*

Prep time: *10 minutes*
Serves 4

Per serving: 300 calories, 10 g fat, 5 g saturated fat, 4 g protein, 18 g carbs, 1 g fiber, 15 g sugar, 53 mg sodium

Tiramimousse

Making mousse is much easier than it seems...just toss, blend, and chill. This recipe is a creamy mousse version of the famous dessert, with a texture and taste to be savored. Dark chocolate is a good source of flavonoids, and we happily justify our dark chocolate addictions with this tidbit of information. Serve with a fruity and floral red wine for a great taste and antioxidant combo.

---

2 (3.5-oz) bars dark bittersweet chocolate such as Valrhona 71% Cacao

4 oz mascarpone cheese (half the container)

1 pint (2 cups) heavy cream or heavy whipping cream

2 tsp instant coffee dissolved in 4 Tbsp hot water

2 Tbsp Marsala wine (just ask a friendly crewmember to point one out)

1   Microwave method to melt chocolate: Break up chocolate bars into squares (8 squares for each bar) and place in a small Pyrex bowl. Microwave for 1 minute and stir. Repeat using 30-second intervals, stirring after every interval until fully melted and waiting a minute between intervals to let the heat of the bowl dissipate. Melting 2 chocolate bars should take about a total of 2 minutes. Be careful not to burn the chocolate.

2   Add mascarpone, cream, coffee, and wine to a blender, adding melted chocolate last. Blend only until mixture thickens (around 10-20 seconds). If you continue blending, the cream will curdle and your guests will cry.

3   Spoon into individual cups and chill in the fridge. If leaving for longer than a couple of hours or making the day before, cover each serving with plastic wrap.

Prep time: *10 minutes. Make at least 2 hours ahead of time.*
Serves 6

Per serving: 565 calories, 52 g fat, 32 g saturated fat, 5 g protein, 20 g carbs, 0 g fiber, 11 g sugar, 28 mg sodium

Wine Suggestion:

Savor this bittersweet
chocolate dessert with sips
of a rich Cabernet such as
Guenoc Cabernet Sauvignon.

Mint Condition Sundae

With Trader Joe's puddings, ice cream, and lemon curd, a quick and yummy sundae dessert is moments away. Mint and fresh strawberries are a perfect pairing with the zing of lemon and the rich pudding flavors. From the crunchy Piroulines on top to the decadent Belgian Chocolate pudding at the bottom, this sundae will be a big hit. Measurements are listed below, but the nice thing about this sundae is just opening a few containers and layering according to your own eye.

¼ cup refrigerated Belgian Chocolate Pudding

½ cup refrigerated Tapioca Pudding

2 Tbsp Lemon Curd

½ cup sliced strawberries (2-3 strawberries) and a few whole for garnish

⅓ cup vanilla ice cream

Fresh mint

2 Pirouline sticks

1   Using a clear glass, begin the layers with chocolate pudding, then half the tapioca, then 1 Tbsp lemon curd, half the strawberries, ice cream, remaining lemon curd, remaining strawberries, and remaining tapioca.

2   Top generously with mint leaves, whole strawberries, and a couple of Pirouline sticks.

Note: *1 jar of Lemon Curd, 2 containers of Tapioca Pudding, 1 container of Belgian Chocolate Pudding, and a box of Pirouline will yield about 8 sundaes.*

Prep time: *5 minutes.*
Serves 1

Per serving: 543 calories, 24 g fat, 15 g saturated fat, 8 g protein, 85 g carbs, 2 g fiber, 64 g sugar, 300 mg sodium

Omit pirouline sticks

All Mixed Up Margaritas

Trader Joe's has a great Margarita Mix, but perhaps you're feeling a little more adventurous. Instead of a mix, try some of the juices we suggest below…pomegranate, pink lemonade, or sparkling lime soda to name a few. There's no substitute for fresh lime in an authentic-tasting margarita, so have plenty on hand; most importantly make sure to pick up a real lime squeezer so your friends will believe you when you claim to be a Margarita master.

¼ cup juice (Organic Pink Lemonade, French Market Limeade, or Just Pomegranate)

½ oz (1 Tbsp) Triple Sec or other orange-flavored liqueur

2 oz (4 Tbsp) tequila (we like Tequila Reserva 1800 Reposado)

2 Tbsp lime juice (juice of 1 lime)

Ice cubes or crushed ice

1   If you want to salt the rim, rub the rim with a cut lime and dip in a shallow dish of kosher or flaked salt. It's also fun using different kinds of sugar to "salt" the rim (such as Turbinado Sugar with the pomegranate version, or Organic Sugar with the Pink Lemonade version).

2   Add ingredients to a glass cup. Add enough ice to fill remainder of cup and stir.

For a small pitcher

1 cup juice (or 1 ½ cups if you don't want it too strong)

¼ cup Triple Sec

1 cup tequila

½ cup lime juice (juice of 4 limes)

3 cups ice

Prep time: 5 minutes
Serves 1 (pitcher serves 4)

Per serving: 218 calories, 0 g fat, 0 g saturated fat, 0 g protein, 16 g carbs, 0 g fiber, 13 g sugar, 0 mg sodium

G Gluten Free   **Vegetarian**

Pound Cake with Berries and Cream

This beautiful dessert is the one you choose for those evenings when you need a one-minute dessert that will please. It's easy to make for one person or for a crowd.

---

1 low-fat tea loaf or pound cake, cut into 1-inch-thick slices

1 cup of prepared whipped cream (in refrigerated canister), divided

4 cups bueberries or other seasonal berries, divided

½ cup Organic Midnight Moo Chocolate Flavored Syrup, divided

1   Place one slice of tea loaf on a plate, top with 2 Tbsp whipped cream, and cover with a handful of berries.

2   Drizzle each dessert with 1 Tbsp syrup.

Prep time: *2 minutes*
Serves 8

Per serving: 253 calories, 8 g fat, 5 g saturated fat, 4 g protein, 42 g carbs, 2 g fiber, 27 g sugar, 77 mg sodium

Almond Pudding

You may never have had a pudding like this before, made only with almond meal and no rice or wheat. A touch of Italian and a touch of Turkish, this pudding is flavored with the great taste and texture of ground almonds and subtle hints of coffee, cinnamon, and vanilla. My sister claims it's even perfect for an indulgent breakfast! Top with whipped cream, Organic Apricot Orange Fruit Spread, or enjoy plain!

2 cups Just Almond Meal (ground almonds)

4 cups whole milk

1 cup sugar

1 tsp cinnamon

1 tsp instant coffee

1 tsp pure vanilla extract

1   Mix all the ingredients in a medium saucepan over medium heat and stir until smooth and even.

2   As it just begins to simmer, turn heat to low and continue stirring occasionally for 20 minutes. The pudding will thicken a little as it cooks, but don't worry if it still looks runny. It will set nicely as it cools.

3   Pour or spoon into small bowls or cups and chill in the fridge for a couple of hours until set. If leaving overnight, cover with plastic wrap.

Cooking time: *20 minutes*
Serves 6

Per serving: 472 calories, 25 g fat, 4 g saturated fat, 15 g protein, 49 g carbs, 4 g fiber, 43 g sugar, 65 mg sodium

Coconut Rice with Mango

This Southeast Asian dessert is a take on Sticky Rice with Mango, which is made with glutinous rice. Our version uses fragrant jasmine rice.

½ cup jasmine rice

½ cup water

1 cup + ¼ cup coconut milk

3 Tbsp sugar

½ cup Mango Sauce or mango nectar (optional)

2 cups sliced mango, such as refrigerated Fresh Cut Mango or frozen Mango Chunks, thawed

1   Combine rice, water, 1 cup coconut milk, and sugar in a saucepan. Bring mixture to a boil. Reduce heat and cover. Simmer over low heat for 30 minutes or until rice is cooked. Remove from heat and let rice sit covered for another 10 minutes.

2   Drizzle 2 Tbsp of mango sauce onto each dessert plate, if using. Place a dollop of coconut rice on center of plate. Top rice with a spoonful of reserved coconut milk, letting it run down the sides. Top with a few slices of mango and serve.

Prep time: *10 minutes*
Hands-off cooking time: *30 minutes*
Serves 4

Per serving: 240 calories, 4 g fat, 3 g saturated fat, 2 g protein, 49 g carbs, 3 g fiber, 22 g sugar, 1 mg sodium

Peachy Sangria

A white version of its classic cousin, Sangria, this peachy version is light and crisp. Make it ahead of time to allow the fruity flavors to meld. This refreshing drink is great for brunch or a light dinner on the patio.

1 bottle dry white wine, such as Barefoot Pinot Grigio

½ cup Montbisou Pêches or other peach liqueur (optional)

2 Tbsp sugar

1-2 peaches, unpeeled and cut into wedges

1 cup assorted colors grapes, halved

1 cup mineral water or club soda

1   Combine wine, liqueur, sugar, and fruit in a glass pitcher. Place in fridge for at least 4 hours.

2   Just before serving, stir in mineral water.

Prep time: 10 minutes
Serves 4

Per serving: 213 calories, 0 g fat, 0 g saturated fat, 1 g protein, 23 g carbs, 1 g fiber, 14 g sugar, 1 mg sodium

Cooking with All Things Trader Joe's

Very Berry Mascarpone Tart

This delightful dessert is a great use of mascarpone cheese, the Italian version of cream cheese. We like the rustic look of colorful berries piled up in no particular order, but of course you could arrange the berries in a symmetrical pattern too. You can skip the crust and make a parfait version by simply layering the filling and berries in a glass. Substitute any fresh fruit you like, such as peaches or figs. Just be sure the fruit is ripe and in season for optimum flavor.

---

1 frozen pie crust, thawed

½ cup heavy whipping cream

¼ cup sugar

1 (8-oz) container mascarpone cheese, softened at room temperature

Pinch salt

1 Tbsp finely grated lemon zest (optional)

1 pint each: fresh raspberries, blueberries, blackberries

1 Preheat oven to 450° F. Defrost the pie crust according to package instructions. Don't forget to let mascarpone cheese soften at room temperature.

2 Press pie crust into a 10-inch tart pan or regular pie pan and cut off excess crust. Prick crust in several places with a fork. For a perfectly shaped crust, place wax paper on top of crust and fill with raw beans or rice. Bake for 15 minutes; remove wax paper and bake 5 minutes longer or until golden brown. If you don't mind more casual-looking crust that may sag in places, simply bake unfilled for 10 minutes. Let crust cool completely.

3 Using an electric mixer, beat heavy cream and sugar until stiff peaks form. Be careful not to over-mix. Stir in mascarpone, salt, and lemon zest. Spread mascarpone mixture evenly on bottom of cooled crust.

4 Arrange berries on top of mascarpone mixture.

Tip: It's best to assemble this tart no more than 2 hours before serving so the crust doesn't get soggy. You can bake the crust and mix the filling ahead of time, leaving everything waiting in the fridge for quick assembly.

Prep time: *15 minutes*
Hands-off cooking time: *10-20 minutes (for crust)*
Serves 8

Per serving: 354 calories, 17 g fat, 10 g saturated fat, 7 g protein,
44 g carbs, 6 g fiber, 16 g sugar, 391 mg sodium

South Seas Chocolate Mousse

Tropical flavors of coconut and rum beckon the pirate in all of us. A few bites and you'll notice your guests starting off sentences with "Arrr," "Ahoy me hearty," and "T'mousse be good." The coconut is subtle and the texture is just as creamy as mousse made with heavy cream. But since light coconut milk has about one sixth of the calories of heavy cream, you won't be adding inches to your pirate booty. Sweet mangoes counterbalance the bittersweet richness of the dark chocolate and add a little bit of color and flair.

Mousse

2 (3.5-oz) bars dark bittersweet chocolate such as Valrhona 71% Cacao

1 (14-oz) can coconut milk

2 Tbsp Captain Morgan Original Spiced Rum (not regular rum)

4 oz mascarpone cheese (½ container)

Topping

2 cups diced mango (fresh or frozen) and/or fresh berries

1   Microwave method to melt chocolate: Break up chocolate bars into squares (8 squares for each bar) and place in a small Pyrex bowl. Microwave for 1 minute and stir. Repeat using 30-second intervals, stirring after every interval until fully melted and waiting a minute between intervals to let the heat of the bowl dissipate. Melting 2 chocolate bars should take about a total of 2 minutes. Be careful not to burn the chocolate.

2   Add coconut milk, rum, and mascarpone cheese to your blender. Pour melted chocolate into blender and blend right away for about 30 seconds. Pour or spoon mousse into individual cups and place in the fridge for at least two hours. If you will be leaving them in the fridge longer than a couple of hours or making it the day before, cover mousse cups with plastic wrap.

3   Top each mousse cup generously with fruit right before serving (about ¼ cup per serving).

Prep time: 5-10 minutes. Make at least 2 hours ahead of time.
Makes 8 (½ -cup) servings

Per serving: 287 calories, 20 g fat, 13 g saturated fat, 3 g protein, 20 g carbs, 1 g fiber, 15 g sugar, 19 mg sodium

Sparkling Pomegranate Cocktail

This festive cocktail is perfect for holiday entertaining. Pomegranate seeds make a colorful and edible garnish. For a non-alcoholic version, use Sparkling Pomegranate Juice instead of champagne and pomegranate juice.

6 tsp fresh Pomegranate Seeds

1 bottle champagne or sparkling wine, chilled

1 cup Just Pomegranate juice, chilled

1   Put 1 tsp pomegranate seeds in each cocktail glass.

2   Combine champagne and pomegranate juice in a pitcher. Pour into cocktail glasses and serve.

Prep time: *5 minutes*
Serves 6

Per serving: 117 calories, 0 g fat, 0 g saturated fat, 0 g protein, 10 g carbs, 0 g fiber, 7 g sugar, 2 mg sodium

Begin with Breakfast

Super-Food Fruit Smoothie

We love a good smoothie as a healthful and easy way to start the day. For the most part, we tend to wing them, but we've found a few favorites we repeat again and again. Kids love smoothies, too, and it's an easy way to experiment with healthy additions for kids and adults alike. This particular smoothie is primarily fruit and yogurt based, but has a few nice additions that round it out. The protein in tofu and yogurt balances out the fruit carbohydrates, and the various textures work to give a nice smooth end result. Flax oil is a viable source of essential fatty acids, and Very Green powder packs a punch of vegetable minerals, vitamins, enzymes, and antioxidants.

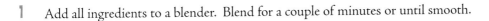

1 ripe banana, peeled

1 cup plain yogurt

½ cup frozen blueberries

1 cup frozen Mango Chunks

⅓ cup soft/regular tofu (about a ¾-inch slice off the end)

1 Tbsp Very Green powdered supplement

2 Tbsp flax oil

1 Tbsp honey

½ cup almond milk or milk of your choice.

1   Add all ingredients to a blender. Blend for a couple of minutes or until smooth.

2   For a delicious smoothie bowl with a little added crunch, pour in a bowl and top with a few Tbsp of granola, such as Granola & the Three Berries, and some fresh berries.

Tip: If you have a popsicle mold, a great way to use leftover smoothies is to make smoothie pops. It's a big hit on summer days!

Prep time: *10 minutes*
Serves 4

Per serving: 219 calories, 9 g fat, 1 g saturated fat, 8 g protein, 29 g carbs, 2 g fiber, 21 g sugar, 59 mg sodium

Dairy-Free Creamy Cashew Smoothie

It's hard to believe there isn't any dairy product in this creamy smoothie. The smooth texture of this fruit and nut-based smoothie comes from cashew butter. And if you're watching your waist, don't be afraid—cashews are actually one of the nuts with the lowest fat content. Furthermore, most of the fat in cashews is oleic acid, which is a heart-healthy monounsaturated fatty acid. Cashews are also a great source of copper, manganese, phosphorus, and magnesium! Mangoes, papaya, and banana are all high in potassium and the antioxidants vitamin A and C, and dates are actually ounce-for-ounce the highest source of antioxidants according to latest studies.

---

1 ripe banana, peeled

2 heaping cups frozen Tropical Fruit Trio or Mango Chunks

1½ cups almond milk or milk of your choice

½ cup cashew butter

2 very soft dates, pitted (optional, don't use if they are very dry)

1 Add all ingredients to a blender.

2 Blend for a couple of minutes or until smooth.

Prep time: *10 minutes*
Serves 4

Per serving: 325 calories, 16 g fat, 3 g saturated fat, 6 g protein,
44 g carbs, 6 g fiber, 28 g sugar, 63 mg sodium

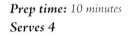

Mushroom Basil Frittata

A frittata is similar to a quiche, but without the crust. You can use virtually any ingredients you have on hand—a great way to use up leftover veggies. This version uses criminis, which are actually baby Portabella mushrooms. They are richer in flavor and nutrients than regular white button mushrooms. For a milder flavor, you can use white button mushrooms or another variety of your choice. This versatile dish can be served around the clock. It's great for breakfast with a warm mug of coffee, or for dinner with a green salad.

3 cups fresh Sliced Crimini Mushrooms

3 Tbsp butter

8 eggs

⅓ cup whole milk or heavy cream

½ tsp salt

¼ tsp black pepper

½ cup fresh basil leaves, roughly chopped

½ cup Quattro Formaggio shredded cheese

1 Preheat oven to 350° F.

2 Melt butter in a 10-inch nonstick oven-safe skillet over medium heat. Add mushrooms and cook for 5 minutes.

3 While mushrooms are cooking, whisk eggs, milk, salt, and pepper until combined. Mix in basil and cheese.

4 Pour egg mixture into hot skillet, over the cooked mushrooms. Place in oven for 30 minutes or until egg is set. Eggs will puff up while cooking but will deflate when you take it out of the oven.

Prep time: *10 minutes*
Hands-off cooking time: *30 minutes*
Serves 6

Per serving: 235 calories, 20 g fat, 10 g saturated fat, 12 g protein, 3 g carbs, 0 g fiber, 1 g sugar, 368 mg sodium

Quick and Creamy Quinoa Cereal

Quinoa (pronounced KEEN-wah) is a nice alternative to oatmeal in the morning; just a little bit is very satisfying. High in protein and gluten free, quinoa is super healthy and has a nice "seedy" texture and a nutty taste. Start with our recipe below and then experiment with your own additions.

1 cup uncooked quinoa, rinsed and drained

2 cups water

½ tsp cinnamon

½ tsp vanilla extract or flavoring

1 ripe banana, peeled and diced

½ cup dried Golden Berry Blend or Dried Berry Medley

¼ cup slivered almonds

1   Add quinoa, water, banana, cinnamon, and vanilla to a small saucepan. Bring to a simmer and cook for 15 minutes or until all the water is absorbed.

2   Mix in nuts and dried berries. Top with cream, milk, honey, Turbinado sugar, or maple syrup as desired.

Prep time: 5 minutes
Hands-off cooking time: 15 minutes
Serves 4

Per serving: 315 calories, 7 g fat, 0 g saturated fat, 8 g protein, 58 g carbs, 6 g fiber, 21 g sugar, 5 mg sodium

Gluten Free   Vegetarian

Orange Cranberry Scones

Perfect for brunch or afternoon tea, these easy scones are light and flaky. Serve with Trader Joe's Lemon Curd for extra flavor. Of course, they're also delicious simply on their own.

3 ½ cups Buttermilk Pancake Mix

3 Tbsp sugar

Zest of 1 orange or 1 Tbsp orange marmalade (optional)

¼ cup unsalted butter, chilled and diced into small squares

¾ cup whole milk

¾ cup dried Orange Flavored Cranberries

1   Preheat oven to 400° F.

2   Mix pancake mix, sugar, and orange zest or marmalade. Add butter and cut into the flour mixture, using a fork or pastry knife, until the butter is the size of peas. (If you have a food processor, it will do this job in just seconds, but it's not necessary.)

3   Add milk and combine. Fold in cranberries. Dough will be quite sticky.

4   Place dough on a well-floured surface. Pat dough into a 4 x 16-inch rectangle; dough will be approximately ¾ inch thick. Cut rectangle into four 4 x 4-inch squares. Cut each square diagonally.

5   Place scones on a cookie sheet and bake for 12 minutes or until golden brown.

Prep time: *15 minutes*
Hands-off cooking time: *12 minutes*
Makes 8 scones

Per scone: 310 calories, 9 g fat, 4 g saturated fat, 5 g protein, 51 g carbs, 1 g fiber, 19 g sugar, 800 mg sodium

Breakfast Crepes

The trick to moist and tender scrambled eggs is to cook them over low heat, while slowly moving them around the pan. Cooking them quickly causes the proteins to bind up, resulting in dry and rubbery eggs. Cooking them slowly allows the curds to form slowly, retaining moisture and remaining slightly creamy. And the crepes couldn't be easier: add water to the mix and you're ready to go!

---

6 ready-made crepes

6 large eggs

½ cup chopped chives

½ tsp salt, ½ tsp pepper

Crème fraîche (optional)

1   Warm crepes according to package instructions. In a medium bowl, add eggs, chives, salt and pepper. Beat with a fork and pour into the same pan, over low heat.

2   When eggs are done, spoon some eggs inside each crepe, spread a little crème fraîche inside, and roll crepes.

Favorite Crepes for breakfast or lunch

⇨ Crumbled Feta, chopped tomato and chopped parsley

⇨ Chopped cooked tail-off shrimp and Pineapple Salsa

⇨ Sliced turkey, Shredded 3 Cheese Blend, and Dried Cranberries

Prep and cooking time: *20 minutes*
Makes 6 crepes

Per crepe: 192 calories, 12 g fat, 2 g saturated fat, 9 g protein, 12 g carbs, 1 g fiber, 4 g sugar, 447 mg sodium

Yogurt Parfait

We really like the crunch and dense goodness of granola in this combination with yogurt and fresh berries, but nearly any cereal will do. If you don't have fresh berries on hand, use Organic Mixed Fruit Spread, a terrific combination of black currant, açai, and pomegranate.

½ cup cup plain yogurt, such as Plain Cream Line Yogurt, or Greek Style Honey Yogurt

¾ cup granola (we like Granola & the 3 Berries or Pecan Praline Granola)

¾ cup fresh berries in season

1 Layer yogurt, granola, and berries in a clear glass, alternating layers a few times.

Prep time: 5 minutes
Serves 1

Per serving: 333 calories, 11 g fat, 4 g saturated fat,
9 g protein, 51 g carbs, 6 g fiber, 24 g sugar, 95 mg sodium

G Gluten Free **V** Vegetarian

Use gluten-free granola,
available in several varieties

Bachelor Quickies
(Complete heat-and-serve menus designed to impress)

Asian Express

Head straight to the frozen foods section for this delicious Asian-inspired feast. Mandarin Orange Chicken is crispy and juicy with a winning sweet and sour flavor. Trader Joe's microwavable rice bags have freshly steamed texture and flavor you would never expect out of a bag. Serve some Asian veggies and crisp egg rolls on the side. For dessert, choose your favorite flavor of Mochi Ice Cream Balls (we like Green Tea).

Dinner

1 (22-oz) bag frozen Mandarin Orange Chicken

1 (30-oz) box frozen Organic Brown or Jasmine Rice (3 bags per box, use 2)

1 (16-oz) bag frozen Asian Vegetables with Beijing Style Soy Sauce

1 pkg frozen Stir Fried Vegetable Egg Rolls (6 egg rolls)

Dessert

1 box frozen Mochi Ice Cream Balls

1 Start chicken first and prepare everything else while chicken cooks.

2 Dessert is ready straight out of the freezer.

Serves 3-4

Cooking with All Things Trader Joe's

Wine Suggestion:

Asian food pairs well with light
fruity wines like Riesling or
Gewürztraminer. Try Joseph
Händler Riesling light and
crisp with citrus flavors.

Naan 'n Curry

If you like spice, this vegetarian meal is for you. "Bhaji" means vegetables in India, and this traditional dish from Bombay is made with potatoes, tomatoes, cauliflower, peas, onions, and spices. A big dollop of yogurt on the side is a cool contrast to the spicy sauce.

Dinner

1 (10.5-oz) box Pav Bhaji, or other selection in the Indian Fare line (Palak Paneer is another of our favorites)

1 box Vegetable Samosas (6 samosas)

1 pkg Tandoori Naan, available in several varieties, or frozen Garlic Naan

Plain yogurt (optional)

Dessert

1 (16-oz) container refrigerated Rice Pudding

1 container refrigerated Fresh Cut Mango

1   Cook samosas according to package instructions; we prefer the oven method.

2   Heat Pav Bhaji in pan or microwave while naan is in the toaster.

3   To assemble dessert, scoop rice pudding into a dish and top with mango slices.

Serves 2

Fancy Italian Night

The chicken in this menu comes stuffed with ricotta and has a package of tasty marinara for pouring over the top. Ready-to-heat fettucini is a breeze to prepare and makes a delicious little pasta dish on the side. Salad doesn't get any easier: salad, toppings, and dressing all in one bag, ready to toss and serve. Profiteroles are small and delicious cream puffs. Drizzle with chocolate sauce included in package.

Dinner

1 pkg refrigerated stuffed chicken breasts of your choice (shelved with raw meats)

1 (16-oz) bag frozen Fettucini With Mushrooms

1 bag A Complete Salad kit (Caesar, Baby Spinach, or Baby Spinach & Mushrooms)

Dessert

1 box frozen Real Italian Cannoli or frozen Tiramisu Torte

1   Put cannoli in the fridge to thaw at the start of dinner. You probably won't need the whole box, but we're not stopping you!

2   Put chicken in the oven and prepare everything else while chicken cooks.

3   Serve the salad as an appetizer or alongside the meal.

Serves 2

Wine Suggestion:

Try a crisp and acidic Pinot Grigio or Pinot Gris (same grape, different geography) with lots of citrus and floral essences such as VINTJS Pinot Gris.

Seafood Soiree

Cioppino is an Italian stew made with seafood simmering in a delicious tomato-based broth. Trader Joe's version is made with scallops, mussels, shrimp, clams, and Alaskan cod. Everything you need is in the bag – just add warm crusty bread for dipping and mopping. One bag serves 2, but if both of you have big appetites, you may need to get two bags and have leftovers for lunch the next day. Crèmes brûlées are impressive, complete in their own ceramic ramekins.

Dinner

1 (16-oz) bag frozen Cioppino Seafood Stew

1 loaf crusty Italian bread

Dessert

1 box frozen Crèmes Brûlées (2 in a pack)

1   While Cioppino is cooking, warm bread in the oven.

2   Use broiler setting in oven to prepare crèmes brûlées.

Serves 2   *Choose gluten-free bread*

Wine Suggestion:

Tres Pinos Tierra Roja, a blend of Merlot, Cabernet Sauvignon, and Syrah, has a ripe berry medley and hints of spice and earth. The earthy quality goes well with fire-roasted asparagus.

Gobble-d-Good Meatloaf

Nourish the body and the soul with a hearty and healthy meal. This ready-made turkey meatloaf is so good, your guests are sure to gobble it up. The portion sizes are generous enough for a double date. Make yourself a meatloaf sandwich with leftovers.

Dinner

1 (24-oz) fully cooked, refrigerated Italian Style Turkey Meatloaf

1 (8-oz) container fully cooked, refrigerated Fire Roasted Asparagus or 1 (12-oz) bag fresh Broccoli Florets (can microwave right in the bag)

1 (24-oz) bag frozen Roasted Potatoes or 2 (16-oz) bags refrigerated Fingerling Potatoes (can microwave right in the bag)

Dessert

1 box frozen Karat Cake or any frozen cheesecake

1   Let Karat Cake thaw on the countertop while you prepare dinner; it needs at least an hour.

2   Meanwhile, cook potatoes according to package instructions, and warm meatloaf and asparagus. If you want to use the oven for everything, cover meatloaf tray with foil and wrap asparagus in foil; place in oven to warm while potatoes are roasting.

Serves 4

Elegant Rack of Lamb

Your dinner guest is sure to be floored with this elegant, restaurant-quality presentation you can throw together in minutes. Perfect for an anniversary, birthday, or a romantic surprise dinner.

Dinner

1 (10-oz) container refrigerated, fully cooked Seasoned Rack of Lamb

1 (10-oz) bag fresh Baby Green Beans

1 (7-oz) bag fresh Sweet Baby Carrots

1 (16-oz) bag fresh Fingerling Potatoes (optional)

1 Tbsp butter

Lemon Pepper seasoning to taste

Dessert

1 box frozen Raspberry Tarte, or frozen Chocolate Ganache Torte

1 Heat lamb according to package instructions; we prefer the oven method.

2 Cook green beans, carrots, and potatoes. Microwaving as suggested on the bags works well. Lightly coat cooked vegetables with butter, and sprinkle with lemon pepper.

3 Thaw dessert according to instructions.

Serves 2-4   *Choose gluten-free dessert*

Wine Suggestion:

For a rich and gamey meat like lamb, go for a Petite Syrah such as **Stag's Leap Winery Petite Syrah**, a big and bold red with deep complexity and chewy tannins.

Good Morning Breakfast

Sleep late—you won't need but a few minutes for this leisurely weekend morning breakfast, perfect for sharing. Crispy and golden French toast, fresh fruit, and a warm cardamom and cinnamon-spiced chai latte are the right way to start off the day. For a bigger breakfast spread, add bacon or breakfast patties.

---

4 slices frozen French Toast

A selection of refrigerated fresh cut fruits

4 frozen Breakfast Patties or 6 slices Fully Cooked Uncured Bacon (optional)

Spicy Chai Latte (powdered mix)

Maple syrup or honey (optional)

1   Heat French toast and bacon or patties according to package directions.

2   Heat water or milk for the chai lattes.

3   Top French toast with syrup or honey and serve with an assortment of fruit on each plate.

Serves 2 *Choose vegetarian sausage patties*

Index

Trader Joe's Store Locations

Arizona

Ahwatukee # 177
4025 E. Chandler Blvd.,
Ste. 38
Ahwatukee, AZ 85048
Phone: 480-759-2295

Glendale # 085
7720 West Bell Road
Glendale, AZ 85308
Phone: 623-776-7414

Mesa # 089
2050 East Baseline Rd.
Mesa, AZ 85204
Phone: 480-632-0951

Paradise Valley # 282
4726 E. Shea Blvd.
Phoenix, AZ 85028
Phone: 602-485-7788

**Phoenix
(Town & Country) # 090**
4821 N. 20th Street
Phoenix, AZ 85016
Phone: 602-912-9022

Scottsdale (North) # 087
7555 E. Frank Lloyd
Wright
N. Scottsdale, AZ 85260
Phone: 480-367-8920

Scottsdale # 094
6202 N. Scottsdale Road
Scottsdale, AZ 85253
Phone: 480-948-9886

Surprise # 092
14095 West Grand Ave.
Surprise, AZ 85374
Phone: 623-546-1640

Tempe # 093
6460 S. McClintock Drive
Tempe, AZ 85283
Phone: 480-838-4142

**Tucson
(Crossroads) # 088**
4766 East Grant Road
Tucson, AZ 85712
Phone: 520-323-4500

**Tucson (Wilmot &
Speedway)# 095**
1101 N. Wilmot Rd.
Suite #147
Tucson, AZ 85712
Phone: 520-733-1313

**Tucson (Campbell &
Limberlost) # 191**
4209 N. Campbell Ave.
Tucson, AZ 85719
Phone: 520-325-0069

Tucson - Oro Valley # 096
7912 N. Oracle
Oro Valley, AZ 85704
Phone: 520-797-4207

California

Agoura Hills
28941 Canwood Street
Agoura Hills, CA 91301
Phone: 818-865-8217

Alameda # 109
2217 South Shore Center
Alameda, CA 94501
Phone: 510-769-5450

Aliso Viejo # 195
The Commons
26541 Aliso Creek Road
Aliso Viejo, CA 92656
Phone: 949-643-5531

Arroyo Grande # 117
955 Rancho Parkway
Arroyo Grande, CA 93420
Phone: 805-474-6114

Bakersfield # 014
8200-C 21 Stockdale Hwy.
Bakersfield, CA 93311
Phone: 661-837-8863

Berkeley #186
1885 University Ave.
Berkeley, CA 94703
Phone: 510-204-9074

Bixby Knolls # 116
4121 Atlantic Ave.
Bixby Knolls, CA 90807
Phone: 562-988-0695

Brea # 011
2500 E. Imperial Hwy.
Suite 177
Brea, CA 92821
Phone 714-257-1180

Brentwood # 201
5451 Lone Tree Way
Brentwood, CA 94513
Phone: 925-516-3044

Burbank # 124
214 East Alameda
Burbank, CA 91502
Phone: 818-848-4299

Camarillo # 114
363 Carmen Drive
Camarillo, CA 93010
Phone: 805-388-1925

Campbell # 073
1875 Bascom Avenue
Campbell, CA 95008
Phone: 408-369-7823

Capitola # 064
3555 Clares Street #D
Capitola, CA 95010
Phone: 831-464-0115

Carlsbad # 220
2629 Gateway Road
Carlsbad, CA 92009
Phone: 760-603-8473

Castro Valley # 084
22224 Redwood Road
Castro Valley, CA 94546
Phone: 510-538-2738

Cathedral City # 118
67-720 East Palm Cyn.
Cathedral City, CA 92234
Phone: 760-202-0090

Cerritos # 104
12861 Towne Center Drive
Cerritos, CA 90703
Phone: 562-402-5148

Chatsworth # 184
10330 Mason Ave.
Chatsworth, CA 91311
Phone: 818-341-3010

Chico # 199
801 East Ave., Suite #110
Chico, CA 95926
Phone: 530-343-9920

Chino Hills # 216
13911 Peyton Dr.
Chino Hills, CA 91709
Phone: 909-627-1404

Chula Vista # 120
878 Eastlake Parkway,
Suite 810
Chula Vista, CA 91914
Phone: 619-656-5370

Claremont # 214
475 W. Foothill Blvd.
Claremont, CA 91711
Phone: 909-625-8784

Clovis # 180
1077 N. Willow, Suite 101
Clovis, CA 93611
Phone: 559-325-3120

**Concord (Oak Grove
& Treat) # 083**
785 Oak Grove Road
Concord, CA 94518
Phone: 925-521-1134

Concord (Airport) # 060
1150 Concord Ave.
Concord, CA 94520
Phone: 925-689-2990

Corona # 213
2790 Cabot Drive, Ste. 165
Corona, CA 92883
Phone: 951-603-0299

Costa Mesa # 035
640 W. 17th Street
Costa Mesa, CA 92627
Phone: 949-642-5134

Culver City # 036
9290 Culver Blvd.
Culver City, CA 90232
Phone: 310-202-1108

Daly City # 074
417 Westlake Center
Daly City, CA 94015
Phone: 650-755-3825

Danville # 065
85 Railroad Ave.
Danville, CA 94526
Phone: 925-838-5757

Davis # 182
885 Russell Blvd.
Davis, CA 95616
Phone: 530-757-2693

Eagle Rock # 055
1566 Colorado Blvd.
Eagle Rock, CA 90041
Phone: 323-257-6422

El Cerrito # 108
225 El Cerrito Plaza
El Cerrito, CA 94530
Phone: 510-524-7609

Elk Grove # 190
9670 Bruceville Road
Elk Grove, CA 95757
Phone: 916-686-9980

Emeryville # 072
5700 Christie Avenue
Emeryville, CA 94608
Phone: 510-658-8091

Encinitas # 025
115 N. El Camino Real,
Suite A
Encinitas, CA 92024
Phone: 760-634-2114

Encino # 056
17640 Burbank Blvd.
Encino, CA 91316
Phone: 818-990-7751

Escondido # 105
1885 So. Centre City
Pkwy., Unit "A"
Escondido, CA 92025
Phone: 760-233-4020

Fair Oaks # 071
5309 Sunrise Blvd.
Fair Oaks, CA 95628
Phone: 916-863-1744

Fairfield # 101
1350 Gateway Blvd.,
Suite A1-A7
Fairfield, CA 94533
Phone: 707-434-0144

Folsom # 172
850 East Bidwell
Folsom, CA 95630
Phone: 916-817-8820

Fremont # 077
39324 Argonaut Way
Fremont, CA 94538
Phone: 510-794-1386

Fresno # 008
5376 N. Blackstone
Fresno, CA 93710
Phone: 559-222-4348

Glendale # 053
130 N. Glendale Ave.
Glendale, CA 91206
Phone: 818-637-2990

Goleta # 110
5767 Calle Real
Goleta, CA 93117
Phone: 805-692-2234

Granada Hills # 044
11114 Balboa Blvd.
Granada Hills, CA 91344
Phone: 818-368-6461

Hollywood
1600 N. Vine Street
Los Angeles, CA 90028
Phone: 323-856-0689

Huntington Bch. # 047
18681-101 Main Street
Huntington Bch., CA
92648
Phone: 714-848-9640

Huntington Bch. # 241
21431 Brookhurst St.
Huntington Bch., CA
92646
Phone: 714-968-4070

Huntington Harbor # 244
Huntington Harbour Mall
16821 Algonquin St.
Huntington Bch.,
CA 92649
Phone: 714-846-7307

**Irvine (Walnut Village
Center) # 037**
14443 Culver Drive
Irvine, CA 92604
Phone: 949-857-8108

**Irvine (University
Center) # 111**
4225 Campus Dr.
Irvine, CA 92612
Phone: 949-509-6138

**Irvine (Irvine &
Sand Cyn) # 210**
6222 Irvine Blvd.
Irvine, CA 92620
Phone: 949-551-6402

La Cañada # 042
475 Foothill Blvd.
La Canada, CA 91011
Phone: 818-790-6373

La Crescenta # 052
3433 Foothill Blvd.
LaCrescenta, CA 91214
Phone: 818-249-3693

La Quinta # 189
46-400 Washington Street
La Quinta, CA 92253
Phone: 760-777-1553

Lafayette # 115
3649 Mt. Diablo Blvd.
Lafayette, CA 94549
Phone: 925-299-9344

Laguna Hills # 039
24321 Avenue De La
Carlota
Laguna Hills, CA 92653
Phone: 949-586-8453

Laguna Niguel # 103
32351 Street of the Golden
Lantern
Laguna Niguel, CA 92677
Phone: 949-493-8599

La Jolla # 020
8657 Villa LaJolla
Drive #210
La Jolla, CA 92037
Phone: 858-546-8629

La Mesa # 024
5495 Grossmont Center
Dr.
La Mesa, CA 91942
Phone: 619-466-0105

Larkspur # 235
2052 Redwood Hwy
Larkspur, CA 94921
Phone: 415-945-7955

Livermore # 208
1122-A East Stanley Blvd.
Livermore, CA 94550
Phone: 925-243-1947

Long Beach (PCH) # 043
6451 E. Pacific Coast Hwy.
Long Beach, CA 90803
Phone: 562-596-4388

**Long Beach
(Bellflower Blvd.) # 194**
2222 Bellflower Blvd.
Long Beach, CA 90815
Phone: 562-596-2514

Los Altos # 127
2310 Homestead Rd.
Los Altos, CA 94024
Phone: 408-245-1917

**Los Angeles
(Silver Lake) # 017**
2738 Hyperion Ave.
Los Angeles, CA 90027
Phone: 323-665-6774

Los Angeles # 031
263 S. La Brea
Los Angeles, CA 90036
Phone: 323-965-1989

**Los Angeles (Sunset Strip)
192**
8000 Sunset Blvd.
Los Angeles, CA 90046
Phone: 323-822-7663

Los Gatos # 181
15466 Los Gatos Blvd.
Los Gatos, CA 95032
Phone 408-356-2324

Manhattan Beach # 034
1821 Manhattan
Beach. Blvd.
Manhattan Bch., CA
90266
Phone: 310-372-1274

Manhattan Beach # 196
1800 Rosecrans Blvd.
Manhattan Beach,
CA 90266
Phone: 310-725-9800

Menlo Park # 069
720 Menlo Avenue
Menlo Park, CA 94025
Phone: 650-323-2134

Millbrae # 170
765 Broadway
Millbrae, CA 94030
Phone: 650-259-9142

Mission Viejo # 126
25410 Marguerite Parkway
Mission Viejo, CA 92692
Phone: 949-581-5638

Modesto # 009
3250 Dale Road
Modesto, CA 95356
Phone: 209-491-0445

Monrovia # 112
604 W. Huntington Dr.
Monrovia, CA 91016
Phone: 626-358-8884

Monterey # 204
570 Munras Ave., Ste. 20
Monterey, CA 93940
Phone: 831-372-2010

Morgan Hill # 202
17035 Laurel Road
Morgan Hill, CA 95037
Phone: 408-778-6409

Mountain View # 081
590 Showers Dr.
Mountain View, CA 94040
Phone: 650-917-1013

Napa # 128
3654 Bel Aire Plaza
Napa, CA 94558
Phone: 707-256-0806

Newbury Park # 243
125 N. Reino Road
Newbury Park, CA
Phone: 805-375-1984

Newport Beach # 125
8086 East Coast Highway
Newport Beach, CA 92657
Phone: 949-494-7404

Novato # 198
7514 Redwood Blvd.
Novato, CA 94945
Phone: 415-898-9359

**Oakland
(Lakeshore) # 203**
3250 Lakeshore Ave.
Oakland, CA 94610
Phone: 510-238-9076

**Oakland
(Rockridge) # 231**
5727 College Ave.
Oakland, CA 94618
Phone: 510-923-9428

Oceanside # 22
2570 Vista Way
Oceanside, CA 92054
Phone: 760-433-9994

Orange # 046
2114 N. Tustin St.
Orange, CA 92865
Phone: 714-283-5697

Pacific Grove # 008
1170 Forest Avenue
Pacific Grove, CA 93950
Phone: 831-656-0180

Palm Desert # 003
44-250 Town Center Way,
Suite C6
Palm Desert, CA 92260
Phone: 760-340-2291

Palmdale # 185
39507 10th Street West
Palmdale, CA 93551
Phone: 661-947-2890

Palo Alto # 207
855 El Camino Real
Palo Alto, CA 94301
Phone: 650-327-7018

**Pasadena
(S. Lake Ave.) # 179**
345 South Lake Ave.
Pasadena, CA 91101
Phone: 626-395-9553

**Pasadena
(S. Arroyo Pkwy.) # 051**
610 S. Arroyo Parkway
Pasadena, CA 91105
Phone: 626-568-9254

**Pasadena
(Hastings Ranch) # 171**
467 Rosemead Blvd.
Pasadena, CA 91107
Phone: 626-351-3399

Petaluma # 107
169 North McDowell Blvd.
Petaluma, CA 94954
Phone: 707-769-2782

Pinole # 230
2742 Pinole Valley Rd.
Pinole, CA 94564
Phone: 510-222-3501

Pleasanton # 066
4040 Pimlico #150
Pleasanton, CA 94588
Phone: 925-225-3600

Rancho Cucamonga # 217
6401 Haven Ave.
Rancho Cucamonga, CA
91737
Phone: 909-476-1410

**Rancho Palos Verdes
057**
28901 S. Western Ave.
#243
Rancho Palos Verdes,
CA 90275
Phone: 310-832-1241

**Rancho Palos Verdes
233**
31176 Hawthorne Blvd.
Rancho Palos Verdes,
CA 90275
Phone: 310-544-1727

**Rancho Santa
Margarita # 027**
30652 Santa Margarita
Pkwy. Suite F102
Rancho Santa Margarita,
CA 92688
Phone: 949-888-3640

Redding # 219
845 Browning St.
Redding, CA 96003
Phone: 530-223-4875

Redlands # 099
552 Orange Street Plaza
Redlands, CA 92374
Phone: 909-798-3888

Redondo Beach # 038
1761 S. Elena Avenue
Redondo Bch., CA 90277
Phone: 310-316-1745

Riverside # 15
6225 Riverside Plaza
Riverside, CA 92506
Phone: 951-682-4684

Roseville # 80
1117 Roseville Square
Roseville, CA 95678
Phone: 916-784-9084

**Sacramento
(Folsom Blvd.) # 175**
5000 Folsom Blvd.
Sacramento, CA 95819
Phone: 916-456-1853

**Sacramento
(Fulton & Marconi) # 070**
2625 Marconi Avenue
Sacramento, CA 95821
Phone: 916-481-8797

San Carlos # 174
1482 El Camino Real
San Carlos, CA 94070
Phone: 650-594-2138

San Clemente # 016
638 Camino DeLosMares,
Sp.#115-G
San Clemente, CA 92673
Phone: 949-240-9996

**San Diego
(Hillcrest) # 026**
1090 University Ste.
G100-107
San Diego, CA 92103
Phone: 619-296-3122

**San Diego
(Point Loma) # 188**
2401 Truxtun Rd., Ste. 300
San Diego, CA 92106
Phone: 619-758-9272

**San Diego
(Pacific Beach) # 021**
1211 Garnet Avenue
San Diego, CA 92109
Phone: 858-272-7235

**San Diego (Carmel Mtn.
Ranch) # 023**
11955 Carmel Mtn. Rd.
#702
San Diego, CA 92128
Phone: 858-673-0526

**San Diego
(Scripps Ranch) # 221**
9850 Hibert Street
San Diego, CA 92131
Phone: 858-549-9185

San Dimas # 028
856 Arrow Hwy. "C"
Target Center
San Dimas, CA 91773
Phone: 909-305-4757

**San Francisco
(9th Street) # 078**
555 9th Street
San Francisco, CA 94103
Phone: 415-863-1292

**San Francisco
(Masonic Ave.) # 100**
3 Masonic Avenue
San Francisco, CA 94118
Phone: 415-346-9964

**San Francisco
(North Beach) # 019**
401 Bay Street
San Francisco, CA 94133
Phone: 415-351-1013

**San Francisco
(Stonestown) # 236**
265 Winston Dr.
San Francisco, CA 94132
Phone: 415-665-1835

San Gabriel # 032
7260 N. Rosemead Blvd.
San Gabriel, CA 91775
Phone: 626-285-5862

San Jose (Bollinger) # 232
7250 Bollinger Rd.
San Jose, CA 95129
Phone: 408-873-7384

**San Jose
(Coleman Ave) # 212**
635 Coleman Ave.
San Jose, CA 95110
Phone: 408-298-9731

**San Jose
(Old Almaden) # 063**
5353 Almaden Expressway
#J-38
San Jose, CA 95118
Phone: 408-927-9091

**San Jose
(Westgate West) # 062**
5269 Prospect
San Jose, CA 95129
Phone: 408-446-5055

San Luis Obispo # 041
3977 Higuera Street
San Luis Obispo, CA
93401
Phone: 805-783-2780

**San Mateo
(Grant Street) # 067**
1820-22 S. Grant Street
San Mateo, CA 94402
Phone: 650-570-6140

**San Mateo
(Hillsdale) # 245**
45 W Hillsdale Blvd
San Mateo, CA 94403
Phone: 650-286-1509

San Rafael # 061
337 Third Street
San Rafael, CA 94901
Phone: 415-454-9530

Santa Ana # 113
3329 South Bristol Street
Santa Ana, CA 92704
Phone: 714-424-9304

**Santa Barbara
(S. Milpas St.) # 059**
29 S. Milpas Street
Santa Barbara, CA 93103
Phone: 805-564-7878

**Santa Barbara
(De La Vina) # 183**
3025 De La Vina
Santa Barbara, CA 93105
Phone: 805-563-7383

Santa Cruz # 193
700 Front Street
Santa Cruz, CA 95060
Phone: 831-425-0140

Santa Maria # 239
1303 S. Bradley Road
Santa Maria, CA 93454
Phone: 805-925-1657

Santa Monica # 006
3212 Pico Blvd.
Santa Monica, CA 90405
Phone: 310-581-0253

**Santa Rosa
(Cleveland Ave.) # 075**
3225 Cleveland Avenue
Santa Rosa, CA 95403
Phone: 707-525-1406

**Santa Rosa
(Santa Rosa Ave.) # 178**
2100 Santa Rosa Ave.
Santa Rosa, CA 95407
Phone: 707-535-0788

Sherman Oaks # 049
14119 Riverside Drive
Sherman Oaks, CA 91423
Phone: 818-789-2771

Simi Valley # 030
2975-A Cochran St.
Simi Valley, CA 93065
Phone: 805-520-3135

South Pasadena # 018
613 Mission Street
South Pasadena, CA 91030
Phone: 626-441-6263

**South San Francisco #
187**
301 McLellan Dr.
So. San Francisco,
CA 94080
Phone: 650-583-6401

Stockton # 076
6535 Pacific Avenue
Stockton, CA 95207
Phone: 209-951-7597

Studio City # 122
11976 Ventura Blvd.
Studio City, CA 91604
Phone: 818-509-0168

Sunnyvale # 068
727 Sunnyvale/
Saratoga Rd.
Sunnyvale, CA 94087
Phone: 408-481-9082

Temecula # 102
40665 Winchester Rd.,
Bldg. B, Ste. 4-6
Temecula, CA 92591
Phone: 951-296-9964

Templeton # 211
1111 Rossi Road
Templeton, CA 93465
Phone: 805-434-9562

Thousand Oaks # 196
451 Avenida
De Los Arboles
Thousand Oaks, CA 91360
Phone: 805-492-7107

Toluca Lake # 054
10130 Riverside Drive
Toluca Lake, CA 91602
Phone: 818-762-2787

**Torrance
(Hawthorne Blvd.) # 121**
19720 Hawthorne Blvd.
Torrance, CA 90503
Phone: 310-793-8585

**Torrance (Rolling
Hills Plaza) # 029**
2545 Pacific Coast
Highway
Torrance, CA 90505
Phone: 310-326-9520

Tustin # 197
12932 Newport Avenue
Tustin, CA 92780
Phone: 714-669-3752

Upland # 010
333 So. Mountain Avenue
Upland, CA 91786
Phone: 909-946-4799

Valencia # 013
26517 Bouquet Canyon Rd
Santa Clarita, CA 91350
Phone: 661-263-3796

Ventura # 045
1795 S. Victoria Avenue
Ventura, CA 93003
Phone: 805-650-9977

Ventura – Midtown
103 S. Mills Road Suite
104
Ventura, CA 93003
Phone: 805-658-2664

Walnut Creek # 123
1372 So. California Blvd.
Walnut Creek, CA 94596
Phone: 925-945-1674

West Hills # 050
6751 Fallbrook Ave.
West Hills, CA 91307
Phone: 818-347-2591

West Hollywood # 040
7304 Santa Monica Blvd.
West Hollywood, CA
90046
Phone: 323-851-9772

West Hollywood # 173
8611 Santa Monica Blvd.
West Hollywood, CA
90069
Phone: 310-657-0152

**West Los Angeles
(National Blvd.) # 007**
10850 National Blvd.
West Los Angeles,
CA 90064
Phone: 310-470-1917

**West Los Angeles
S. Sepulveda Blvd.) # 119**
3456 S. Sepulveda Blvd.
West Los Angeles,
CA 90034
Phone: 310-836-2458

**West Los Angeles
(Olympic) # 215**
11755 W. Olympic Blvd.
West Los Angeles,
CA 90064
Phone: 310-477-5949

Westchester # 033
8645 S. Sepulveda
Westchester, CA 90045
Phone: 310-338-9238

Westlake Village # 058
3835 E. Thousand
Oaks Blvd.
Westlake Village, CA
91362
Phone: 805-494-5040

Westwood # 234
1000 Glendon Avenue
Los Angeles, CA 90024
Phone: 310-824-1495

Whittier # 048
15025 E. Whittier Blvd.
Whittier, CA 90603
Phone: 562-698-1642

Woodland Hills # 209
21054 Clarendon St.
Woodland Hills, CA 91364
Phone: 818-712-9475

Yorba Linda # 176
19655 Yorba Linda Blvd.
Yorba Linda, CA 92886
Phone: 714-970-0116

Connecticut

Danbury # 525
113 Mill Plain Rd.
Danbury, CT 06811
Phone: 203-739-0098
Alcohol: Beer Only

Darien # 522
436 Boston Post Rd.
Darien, CT 06820
Phone: 203-656-1414
Alcohol: Beer Only

Fairfield # 523
2258 Black Rock Turnpike
Fairfield, CT 06825
Phone: 203-330-8301
Alcohol: Beer Only

Orange # 524
560 Boston Post Road
Orange, CT 06477
Phone: 203-795-5505
Alcohol: Beer Only

West Hartford # 526
1489 New Britain Ave.
West Hartford, CT 06110
Phone: 860-561-4771
Alcohol: Beer Only

Westport # 521
400 Post Road East
Westport, CT 06880
Phone: 203-226-8966
Alcohol: Beer Only

Delaware

Wilmington* # 536
5605 Concord Pike
Wilmington, DE 19803
Phone: 302-478-8494

District of Columbia

Washington # 653
1101 25th Street NW
Washington, DC 20037
Phone: 202-296-1921

Georgia

Athens
1850 Epps Bridge Parkway
Athens, GA 30606
Phone: 706-583-8934

**Atlanta
(Buckhead) # 735**
3183 Peachtree Rd NE
Atlanta, GA 30305
Phone: 404-842-0907

Atlanta (Midtown) # 730
931 Monroe Dr., NE
Atlanta, GA 30308
Phone: 404-815-9210

Marietta # 732
4250 Roswell Road
Marietta, GA 30062
Phone: 678-560-3585

Norcross # 734
5185 Peachtree Parkway,
Bld. 1200
Norcross, GA 30092
Phone: 678-966-9236

Roswell # 733
635 W. Crossville Road
Roswell, GA 30075
Phone: 770-645-8505

Sandy Springs # 731
6277 Roswell Road NE
Sandy Springs, GA 30328
Phone: 404-236-2414

Illinois

Algonquin # 699
1800 South Randall Road
Algonquin, IL 60102
Phone: 847-854-4886

Arlington Heights # 687
17 W. Rand Road
Arlington Heights,
IL 60004
Phone: 847-506-0752

Batavia # 689
1942 West Fabyan
Parkway #222
Batavia, IL 60510
Phone: 630-879-3234

**Chicago
River North) # 696**
44 E. Ontario St.
Chicago, IL 60611
Phone: 312-951-6369

**Chicago
(Lincoln & Grace) # 688**
3745 North Lincoln
Avenue
Chicago, IL 60613
Phone: 773-248-4920
**Chicago
(Lincoln Park) # 691**
1840 North Clybourn
Avenue #200
Chicago, IL 60614
Phone: 312-274-9733

*Chicago (South Loop) –
coming soon!*
1147 S. Wabash Ave.
Chicago, IL 60605
Phone: TBD

*Chicago (Lakeview) –
coming soon!*`
667 W. Diversey Pkwy
Chicago, IL 60614
Phone: 773-935-7255

Downers Grove # 683
122 Ogden Ave.
Downers Grove, IL 60515
Phone: 630-241-1662

Glen Ellyn # 680
680 Roosevelt Rd.
Glen Ellyn, IL 60137
Phone: 630-858-5077

Glenview # 681
1407 Waukegan Road
Glenview, IL 60025
Phone: 847-657-7821

La Grange # 685
25 North La Grange Road
La Grange, IL 60525
Phone: 708-579-0838

Lake Zurich # 684
735 W. Route 22**
Lake Zurich, IL 60047
Phone: 847-550-7827
[**For accurate driving directions using GPS, please
use 735 W Main Street]

Naperville # 690
44 West Gartner Road
Naperville, IL 60540
Phone: 630-355-4389

Northbrook # 682
127 Skokie Blvd.
Northbrook, IL 60062
Phone: 847-498-9076

Oak Park # 697
483 N. Harlem Ave.
Oak Park, IL 60301
Phone: 708-386-1169

Orland Park # 686
14924 S. La Grange Road
Orland Park, IL 60462
Phone: 708-349-9021

Park Ridge # 698
190 North Northwest
Highway
Park Ridge, IL 60068
Phone: 847-292-1108

Indiana

Indianapolis (Castleton) # 671
5473 East 82nd Street
Indianapolis, IN 46250
Phone: 317-595-8950

Indianapolis (West 86th) # 670
2902 West 86th Street
Indianapolis, IN 46268
Phone: 317-337-1880

Iowa

West Des Moines
6305 Mills Civic Parkway
West Des Moines, IA 50266
Phone: 515-225-3820

Kansas–

Coming Soon!

Leawood – coming soon!
4201 W 119th Street
Leawood, KS 66209
Phone: TBD

Maine

Portland
87 Marginal Way
Portland, ME 04101
Phone: 207-699-3799

Maryland

Annapolis* # 650
160 F Jennifer Road
Annapolis, MD 21401
Phone: 410-573-0505

Bethesda* # 645
6831 Wisconsin Avenue
Bethesda, MD 20815
Phone: 301-907-0982

Columbia* # 658
6610 Marie Curie Dr.
(Int. of 175 & 108)
Elkridge, MD 21075
Phone: 410-953-8139

Gaithersburg* # 648
18270 Contour Rd.
Gaithersburg, MD 20877
Phone: 301-947-5953

Pikesville* # 655
1809 Reisterstown Road, Suite #121
Pikesville, MD 21208
Phone: 410-484-8373

Rockville* # 642
12268-H Rockville Pike
Rockville, MD 20852
Phone: 301-468-6656

Silver Spring* # 652
10741 Columbia Pike
Silver Spring, MD 20901
Phone: 301-681-1675

Towson* # 649
1 E. Joppa Rd.
Towson, MD 21286
Phone: 410-296-9851

Massachusetts

Acton* # 511
145 Great Road
Acton, MA 01720
Phone: 978-266-8908

Arlington* # 505
1427 Massachusetts Ave.
Arlington, MA 02476
Phone: 781-646-9138

Boston #510
899 Boylston Street
Boston, MA 02115
Phone: 617-262-6505

Brookline # 501
1317 Beacon Street
Brookline, MA 02446
Phone: 617-278-9997

Burlington* # 515
51 Middlesex Turnpike
Burlington, MA 01803
Phone: 781-273-2310

Cambridge
748 Memorial Drive
Cambridge, MA 02139
Phone: 617-491-8582

Cambridge (Fresh Pond)* # 517
211 Alewife Brook Pkwy
Cambridge, MA 02138
Phone: 617-498-3201

Framingham # 503
659 Worcester Road
Framingham, MA 01701
Phone: 508-935-2931

Hadley* # 512
375 Russell Street
Hadley, MA 01035
Phone: 413-587-3260

Hanover* # 513
1775 Washington Street
Hanover, MA 02339
Phone: 781-826-5389

Hyannis* # 514
Christmas Tree Promenade
655 Route 132, Unit 4-A
Hyannis, MA 02601
Phone: 508-790-3008

Needham Hts* 504
958 Highland Avenue
Needham Hts, MA 02494
Phone: 781-449-6993

Peabody* # 516
300 Andover Street, Suite 15
Peabody, MA 01960
Phone: 978-977-5316

Saugus* # 506
358 Broadway, Unit B
(Shops @ Saugus, Rte. 1)
Saugus, MA 01906
Phone: 781-231-0369

Shrewsbury* # 508
77 Boston Turnpike
Shrewsbury, MA 01545
Phone: 508-755-9560

Tyngsboro* # 507
440 Middlesex Road
Tyngsboro, MA 01879
Phone: 978-649-2726

West Newton* # 509
1121 Washington St.
West Newton, MA 02465
Phone: 617-244-1620

Michigan

Ann Arbor # 678
2398 East Stadium Blvd.
Ann Arbor, MI 48104
Phone: 734-975-2455

Farmington Hills # 675
31221 West 14 Mile Road
Farmington Hills, MI 48334
Phone: 248-737-4609

Grosse Pointe # 665
17028 Kercheval Ave.
Grosse Pointe, MI 48230
Phone: 313-640-7794

Northville # 667
20490 Haggerty Road
Northville, MI 48167
Phone: 734-464-3675

Rochester Hills # 668
3044 Walton Blvd.
Rochester Hills, MI 48309
Phone: 248-375-2190

Royal Oak # 674
27880 Woodward Ave.
Royal Oak, MI 48067
Phone: 248-582-9002

Minnesota

Maple Grove # 713
12105 Elm Creek Blvd. N.
Maple Grove, MN 55369
Phone: 763-315-1739

Minnetonka # 714
11220 Wayzata Blvd
Minnetonka, MN 55305
Phone: 952-417-9080

Rochester
1200 16th St. SW
Rochester, NY 55902
Phone: 952-417-9080

St. Louis Park # 710
4500 Excelsior Blvd.
St. Louis Park, MN 55416
Phone: 952-285-1053

St. Paul # 716
484 Lexington Parkway S.
St. Paul, MN 55116
Phone: 651-698-3119

Woodbury # 715
8960 Hudson Road
Woodbury, MN 55125
Phone: 651-735-0269

Missouri

Brentwood # 792
48 Brentwood
Promenade Court
Brentwood, MO 63144
Phone: 314-963-0253

Chesterfield # 693
1679 Clarkson Road
Chesterfield, MO 63017
Phone: 636-536-7846

Creve Coeur # 694
11505 Olive Blvd.
Creve Coeur, MO 63141
Phone: 314-569-0427

Des Peres # 695
13343 Manchester Rd.
Des Peres, MO 63131
Phone: 314-984-5051

Kansas City – coming soon!
8600 Ward Parkway
Kansas City, MO 64114
Phone: TBD

Nebraska

Lincoln
3120 Pine Lake Road, Suite R
Lincoln, NE 68516
Phone: 402-328-0120

Omaha # 714
10305 Pacific St.
Omaha, NE 68114
Phone: 402-391-3698

Nevada

Anthem # 280
10345 South Eastern Ave.
Henderson, NV 89052
Phone: 702-407-8673

Carson City # 281
3790 US Highway 395 S, Suite 401
Carson City, NV 89705
Phone: 775-267-2486

Henderson # 097
2716 North Green Valley Parkway
Henderson, NV 89014
Phone: 702-433-6773

Las Vegas (Decatur Blvd.) # 098
2101 S. Decatur Blvd., Suite 25
Las Vegas, NV 89102
Phone: 702-367-0227

Las Vegas (Summerlin) # 086
7575 West Washington, Suite 117
Las Vegas, NV 89128
Phone: 702-242-8240

Reno # 082
5035 S. McCarran Blvd.
Reno, NV 89502
Phone: 775-826-1621

New Jersey

Edgewater* # 606
715 River Road
Edgewater, NJ 07020
Phone: 201-945-5932

Florham Park* # 604
186 Columbia Turnpike
Florham Park, NJ 07932
Phone: 973-514-1511

Marlton* # 631
300 P Route 73 South
Marlton, NJ 08053
Phone: 856-988-3323

Millburn* # 609
187 Millburn Ave.
Millburn, NJ 07041
Phone: 973-218-0912

Paramus* # 605
404 Rt. 17 North
Paramus, NJ 07652
Phone: 201-265-9624

Princeton # 607
3528 US 1
(Brunswick Pike)
Princeton, NJ 08540
Phone: 609-897-0581

Shrewsbury*
1031 Broad St.
Shrewsbury, NJ 07702
Phone: 732-389-2535

Wayne* # 632
1172 Hamburg Turnpike
Wayne, NJ 07470
Phone: 973-692-0050

Westfield # 601
155 Elm St.
Westfield, NJ 07090
Phone: 908-301-0910

Westwood* # 602
20 Irvington Street
Westwood, NJ 07675
Phone: 201-263-0134

New Mexico

Albuquerque # 166
8928 Holly Ave. NE
Albuquerque, NM 87122
Phone: 505-796-0311

Albuquerque (Uptown) # 167
2200 Uptown Loop NE
Albuquerque, NM 87110
Phone: 505-883-3662

Santa Fe # 165
530 W. Cordova Road
Santa Fe, NM 87505
Phone: 505-995-8145

New York

Brooklyn # 558
130 Court St
Brooklyn, NY 11201
Phone: 718-246-8460
Alcohol: Beer Only

Commack # 551
5010 Jericho Turnpike
Commack, NY 11725
Phone: 631-493-9210
Alcohol: Beer Only

Hartsdale # 533
215 North Central Avenue
Hartsdale, NY 10530
Phone: 914-997-1960
Alcohol: Beer Only

Hewlett # 554
1280 West Broadway
Hewlett, NY 11557
Phone: 516-569-7191
Alcohol: Beer Only

Lake Grove # 556
137 Alexander Ave.
Lake Grove, NY 11755
Phone: 631-863-2477
Alcohol: Beer Only

Larchmont # 532
1260 Boston Post Road
Larchmont, NY 10538
Phone: 914-833-9110
Alcohol: Beer Only

Merrick # 553
1714 Merrick Road
Merrick, NY 11566
Phone: 516-771-1012
Alcohol: Beer Only

**New York
(72nd & Broadway) # 542**
2075 Broadway
New York, NY 10023
Phone: 212-799-0028
Alcohol: Beer Only

**New York
(Chelsea) # 543**
675 6th Ave
New York, NY 10010
Phone: 212-255-2106
Alcohol: Beer Only

**New York (Union Square
Grocery) # 540**
142 E. 14th St.
New York, NY 10003
Phone: 212-529-4612
Alcohol: Beer Only

**New York (Union Square
Wine) # 541**
138 E. 14th St.
New York, NY 10003
Phone: 212-529-6326
Alcohol: Wine Only

Oceanside # 552
3418 Long Beach Rd.
Oceanside, NY 11572
Phone: 516-536-9163
Alcohol: Beer Only

Plainview # 555
425 S. Oyster Bay Rd.
Plainview, NY 11803
Phone: 516-933-6900
Alcohol: Beer Only

Queens # 557
90-30 Metropolitan Ave.
Queens, NY 11374
Phone: 718-275-1791
Alcohol: Beer Only

Scarsdale # 531
727 White Plains Rd.
Scarsdale, NY 10583
Phone: 914-472-2988
Alcohol: Beer Only

*Staten Island
– coming soon!*
2385 Richmond Ave
Staten Island, NY 10314
Phone: TBD
Alcohol: Beer Only

North Carolina
Cary # 741
1393 Kildaire Farms Rd.
Cary, NC 27511
Phone: 919-465-5984

Chapel Hill # 745
1800 E. Franklin St.
Chapel Hill, NC 27514
Phone: 919-918-7871

**Charlotte
(Midtown) # 744**
1133 Metropolitan Ave.,
Ste. 100
Charlotte, NC 28204
Phone: 704-334-0737

Charlotte (North) # 743
1820 East Arbors Dr.**
(corner of W. Mallard
Creek Church Rd. & Sena-
tor Royall Dr.)
Charlotte, NC 28262
Phone: 704-688-9578
[**For accurate driving
directions on the web,
please use 1820 W. Mallard
Creek Church Rd.]

Charlotte (South) # 742
6418 Rea Rd.
Charlotte, NC 28277
Phone: 704-543-5249

Raleigh # 746
3000 Wake Forest Rd.
Raleigh, NC 27609
Phone: 919-981-7422

Ohio
Cincinnati # 669
7788 Montgomery Road
Cincinnati, OH 45236
Phone: 513-984-3452

Columbus # 679
3888 Townsfair Way
Columbus, OH 43219
Phone: 614-473-0794

Dublin # 672
6355 Sawmill Road
Dublin, OH 43017
Phone: 614-793-8505

Kettering # 673
328 East Stroop Road
Kettering, OH 45429
Phone: 937-294-5411

Westlake # 677
175 Market Street
Westlake, OH 44145
Phone: 440-250-1592

Woodmere # 676
28809 Chagrin Blvd.
Woodmere, OH 44122
Phone: 216-360-9320

Oregon
Beaverton # 141
11753 S. W. Beaverton
Hillsdale Hwy.
Beaverton, OR 97005
Phone: 503-626-3794

Bend # 150
63455 North
Highway 97, Ste. 4
Bend, OR 97701
Phone: 541-312-4198

Clackamas # 152
9345 SE 82nd Ave
(across from Home Depot)
Happy Valley, OR 97086

Phone: 503-771-6300
Corvallis # 154
1550 NW 9th Street
Corvallis, OR 97330
Phone: 541-753-0048

Eugene # 145
85 Oakway Center
Eugene, OR 97401
Phone: 541-485-1744

Hillsboro # 149
2285 NW 185th Ave.
Hillsboro, OR 97124
Phone: 503-645-8321

Lake Oswego # 142
15391 S. W. Bangy Rd.
Lake Oswego, OR 97035
Phone: 503-639-3238

Portland (SE) # 143
4715 S. E. 39th Avenue
Portland, OR 97202
Phone: 503-777-1601

Portland (NW) # 146
2122 N.W. Glisan
Portland, OR 97210
Phone: 971-544-0788

**Portland
(Hollywood) # 144**
4121 N.E. Halsey St.
Portland, OR 97213
Phone: 503-284-1694

Salem – coming soon!
4450 Commercial St.,
Suite 100
Salem, OR 97302
Phone: TBD

Pennsylvania
Ardmore* # 635
112 Coulter Avenue
Ardmore, PA 19003
Phone: 610-658-0645

Jenkintown* # 633
933 Old York Road
Jenkintown, PA 19046
Phone: 215-885-524

Media* # 637
12 East State Street
Media, PA 19063
Phone: 610-891-2752

North Wales* # 639
1430 Bethlehem Pike
(corner SR 309 & SR 63)
North Wales, PA 19454
Phone: 215-646-5870

Philadelphia* # 634
2121 Market Street
Philadelphia, PA 19103
Phone: 215-569-9282

Pittsburgh* # 638
6343 Penn Ave.
Pittsburgh, PA 15206
Phone: 412-363-5748

Pittsburgh
- coming soon!*
1600 Washington Road
Pittsburgh, PA 15228
Phone: TBD

Wayne* # 632
171 East Swedesford Rd.
Wayne, PA 19087
Phone: 610-225-0925

Rhode Island
Warwick* # 518
1000 Bald Hill Rd
Warwick, RI 02886
Phone: 401-821-5368

South Carolina
Greenville
59 Woodruff
Industrial Lane
Greenville, SC 29607
Phone: 864-286-0231

*Mt. Pleasant –
coming soon!*
401 Johnnie Dodds Blvd.
Mt. Pleasant, SC 29464
Phone: TBD

Tennessee
Nashville # 664
3909 Hillsboro Pike
Nashville, TN 37215
Phone: 615-297-6560
Alcohol: Beer Only

Virginia
Alexandria # 647
612 N. Saint Asaph Street
Alexandria, VA 22314
Phone: 703-548-0611

Bailey's Crossroads # 644
5847 Leesburg Pike
Bailey's Crossroads,
VA 22041
Phone: 703-379-5883

Centreville # 654
14100 Lee Highway
Centreville, VA 20120
Phone: 703-815-0697

Fairfax # 643
9464 Main Street
Fairfax, VA 22031
Phone: 703-764-8550

Falls Church # 641
7514 Leesburg Turnpike
Falls Church, VA 22043
Phone: 703-288-0566

Newport News # 656
12551 Jefferson Ave.,
Suite #179
Newport News, VA 23602
Phone: 757-890-0235

Reston # 646
11958 Killingsworth Ave.
Reston, VA 20194
Phone: 703-689-0865

**Richmond
(Short Pump) # 659**
11331 W Broad St, Ste 161
Glen Allen, VA 23060
Phone: 804-360-4098

Springfield # 651
6394 Springfield Plaza
Springfield, VA 22150
Phone: 703-569-9301

Virginia Beach # 660
503 Hilltop Plaza
Virginia Beach, VA 23454
Phone: 757-422-4840

Williamsburg # 657
5000 Settlers Market Blvd
(corner of Monticello and
Settlers Market)**
Williamsburg, VA 23188
Phone: 757-259-2135
[**For accurate driving
directions on the web, please
use 5224 Monticello Ave.]

Washington
Ballard # 147
4609 14th Avenue NW
Seattle, WA 98107
Phone: 206-783-0498

Bellevue # 131
15400 N. E. 20th Street
Bellevue, WA 98007
Phone: 425-643-6885

Bellingham # 151
2410 James Street
Bellingham, WA 98225
Phone: 360-734-5166

Burien # 133
15868 1st. Avenue South
Burien, WA 98148
Phone: 206-901-9339

Everett # 139
811 S.E. Everett Mall Way
Everett, WA 98208
Phone: 425-513-2210

Federal Way # 134
1758 S. 320th Street
Federal Way, WA 98003
Phone: 253-529-9242

Issaquah # 138
1495 11th Ave. N.W.
Issaquah, WA 98027
Phone: 425-837-8088

Kirkland # 132
12632 120th Avenue N. E.
Kirkland, WA 98034
Phone: 425-823-1685

Lynnwood # 129
19500 Highway 99,
Suite 100
Lynnwood, WA 98036
Phone: 425-744-1346

Olympia # 156
Olympia West Center
1530 Black Lake Blvd.
Olympia, WA 98502
Phone: 360-352-7440

Redmond # 140
15932 Redmond Way
Redmond, WA 98052
Phone: 425-883-1624

Seattle (U. District) # 137
4555 Roosevelt Way NE
Seattle, WA 98105
Phone: 206-547-6299

**Seattle
(Queen Anne Hill) # 135**
112 West Galer St.
Seattle, WA 98119
Phone: 206-378-5536

Seattle
(Capitol Hill) # 130
1700 Madison St.
Seattle, WA 98122
Phone: 206-322-7268

Spokane – coming soon!
2975 East 29th Avenue
Spokane, WA 99223
Phone: TBD

University Place # 148
3800 Bridgeport Way West
University Place, WA 98466
Phone: 253-460-2672

Vancouver # 136
305 SE Chkalov Drive #B1
Vancouver, WA 98683
Phone: 360-883-9000

Wisconsin

Glendale # 711
5600 North Port
Washington Road
Glendale, WI 53217
Phone: 414-962-3382

Madison # 712
1810 Monroe Street
Madison, WI 53711
Phone: 608-257-1916

Other titles in this cookbook series:

Cooking with Trader Joe's: Companion
by **Deana Gunn & Wona Miniati**
ISBN 978-0-9799384-9-8

Cooking with Trader Joe's: Dinner's Done!
by **Deana Gunn & Wona Miniati**
ISBN 978-0-9799384-3-6

Cooking with Trader Joe's: Pack A Lunch!
by **Céline Cossou-Bordes**
ISBN 978-0-9799384-5-0

Cooking with Trader Joe's: Skinny Dish!
by **Jennifer K. Reilly, RD**
ISBN 978-0-9799384-7-4

Cooking with Trader Joe's: Lighten Up!
by **Susan Greeley, MS, RD**
ISBN 978-0-9799384-6-7

**Available everywhere books are sold.
Please visit us at**

CookTJ.com

Photo Credits

By **shutterstock.com**: Cover, back cover: © Allgusak © axle71 © OtnaYdur © Rosamund Parkinson © Elisanth © Polina Katritch © Labetskiy Alexandr Alexandrovich © Eric Isselée © Elena Schweitzer © Jovan Nikolic © Rosamund Parkinson © 100ker / Pages: 12, 42, 43, 84, 124, 174, 175, 180, 199, 208, 230, 247 © 100ker / 3, 133, 164, 182, 258 © AJP / 191 © Aaron Amat / 13, 219 © AddyTsl / 3, 21, 59, 83, 141, 148, 167, 215, 235, 247 © Alegria / 23 © Alex Staroseltsev / 1 © Allgusak / 185 © Alexander Dashewsky / 134 © Andris Tkacenko / 42, 92, 116, 199, 229, 230, 231, 245 © Andrjuss / 31, 60, 140 © Angel Simon / 41, 230 © aquariagirl1970 / 43, 254 © Artspace / 195, 231 © axle71 / 236 © B.G. Smith / 236 © Bassittart / 46, 175, 199, 204, 209, 236, 245 © beboy / 198 © billybear / 49 © Black Rock Digital / 6, 224, 231 © BlankaB / 19 © Bomshtein / 41 © bonchan / 52, 147, 159, 178, 191 © Borat / 1, 51, 84 © Brenda Carson / 182 © Brooke Becker / 63 © Cameramannz / 246 © Carlos Caetano / 15 © Carlos Restrepo / 257 © Chiyacat / 56 © Chris Howey / 42 © Chuck Wagner / 12 © CLM / 85, 252 © Daniel Padavona / 261 © Daniel Wiedemann / 242 © Dimitar Bosakov / 55, 188 © dionisvera / 31, 95 © Dmitriy Shironosov / 79, 87, 136, 152, 222, 247 © Elaine Barker / 99 © Elena Elisseeva / 92 © elena moiseeva / 12, 24, 32, 42, 45, 72, 107, 147, 167, 174, 230, 231, 257 © Elena Schweitzer / 3, 12, 80, 107, 177, 198, 216, 247 © Elisanth / 129 © Emily Sartoski / 116, 130 © enciktat / 64, 124, 156, 174, 246 © Eric Gevaert / 198 © Eric Isselée / 164 © Fedorov Oleksiy / 56 © Feng Yu / 238 © Frank Oppermann / 52 © Garsya / 222 © gresei / 26 © Gudrun Muenz / 203 © guysal / 80 © Halina Yakushevich / 175, 247 © hans.slegers / 179 © haveseen / 82 © Hintau Aliaksei / 148, 254 © Hintau Aliaksei / 96 © Iain McGillivray / 174 160 © ifong / © Iakov Kalinin / 210 © Irena Misevic / 36, 163 © Ivaschenko Roman / 13 © javarman / 95 © jcjgphotography / 11, 186, 201, 203, 221, 248 © jennyz / 170 © Jiang Hongyan / 87, 88, 111, 221 © Jiri Hera / 180 © Joerg Beuge / 12, 198 © Jovan Nikolic / 231 © Judy Tejero / 38 © Kai Wong / 16 © Kelly Richardson / 75 © kiboka / 123 © Komar Maria / 49, 144 © Kulish Viktoriia / 8, 13, 38, 43, 231 © Kynata / 1, 7, 9, 36, 72, 76, 98, 123, 185, © Labetskiy Alexandr Alexandrovich / 1, 13, 67, 89, 243 © Le Do / 59 © Lisovskaya Natalia / 233 © Ljupco Smokovski / 79 © LubaShi / 158 © Luiz Rocha / 209, 226 © M. Unal Ozmen / 241 © Madlen / 50 © Margrit Hirsch / 95 © Mark Stout Photography / 12 © Mark Winfrey / 206 © matin / 1, 42, 85, 175, 231 © Maugli / 91 © maya13 / 68 © Mazzzur / 111, 198, 204 © Megan Gayle / 12 © Nenilkime / 192 © niderlander / 46 © Nikola Bilic / 103 © Noraluca013 / 13, 188, 231, 251 © OtnaYdur / 35 © Pamela Uyttendaele / 198 © pashabo / 136 © Peter zijlstra / 248 © Picsfive / 1, 43, 100, 123, 241 © Polina Katritch / 130 © ravl / 195 © ryby / 19, 177, 261 © Rosamund Parkinson / 261 © Ruslan Ivantsov / 154 © saiko3p / 252 © Sally Scott / 85 © Sandra Cunningham / 108 © sarsmis / 16, 105, 143, 168 © Serhiy Shullye / 20, 198 © Skyline / 55, 67, 139, 154, 186, 212, © Spyder / 212 © Stefanie Mohr Photography / 42, 245 © Stephanie Swartz / 96 © Sushkin / 258 © Tamara Kulikova / 8, 144 © TeddyandMia / 76 © Teresa Azevedo / 12 © thatsmymop / 246 © Triff / 105, 230 © Vakhrushev Pavel / 28, 219 © Valentyn Volkov / 4, 15 © Videowokart / 246 © Viktar Malyshchyts / 11, 32 © Viktoria / 186 © Volosina / 163, 168, 170, 198, 199, 231 © vso / 127 © WilleeCole / 80, 152, 206 © Yasonya / 85 © zolssa

By **Clipart ETC** © 2011 University of South Florida, illustrations on pages: 1, 13, 25, 26, 45, 68, 75, 85, 91, 103, 112, 119, 129, 160, 173, 175, 198, 199, 246.

All other llustrations © **Dover Publications, Inc.** on pages: Cover, back cover, 1, 133